DO ASK, DO TELL: WHEN LIBERTY IS STRESSED

DO ASK, DO TELL: WHEN LIBERTY IS STRESSED

Updates to Bill of Rights II; Essays on Challenges to Free Speech and to Other Liberties

Bill Boushka

Writers Club Press
New York   Lincoln   Shanghai

Do Ask, Do Tell: When Liberty Is Stressed
Updates to Bill of Rights II;
Essays on Challenges to Free Speech and to Other Liberties

Writers Club Press
an imprint of iUniverse, Inc.

For information address:
iUniverse
2021 Pine Lake Road, Suite 100
Lincoln, NE 68512
www.iuniverse.com

ISBN: 0-595-26059-4

Printed in the United States of America

CONTENTS

PREFACE

This book is primarily intended to update the vision in *Do Ask, Do Tell: A Gay Conservative Lashes Back* (1997, 2000) given the new challenges to liberty posed particularly by terrorism and now corporate scandals, as well as the growing understanding of the legal and ethical problems that accompany the opportunities for self-expression presented by the Internet.

In 1998 I wrote a short booklet, *Our Fundamental Rights and How We Can Reclaim Them* as a lay person's conceptual guide to individual rights. This little work was intended as a high-level summary of the material in *Do Ask, Do Tell*. In 1999 I wrote a more formal proposal with an essay, "Bill of Rights II," and that has been posted on my hppub.com website since then. In September 2002 I printed that essay in a monograph *Bill of Rights 2 and Other Topics*. This new book replaces that 2000 publication with a brief work that I believe necessary particularly in the aftermath of the 9-11-2001 tragedy.

The long essay on terrorism is intended to review the breach in the "firewall" between government and civil liberties, a barrier that I had spent these years proposing. The remaining essays explore various aspects of liberty and self-expression as they have evolved in the past few years. The chapter on the Child Online Protection Act (COPA), against which I am a litigant, discusses balancing Internet freedom of expression and protecting children. The discussion of self-publishing explores the potential ethical and legal problems as new writers and artists take advantage of the new technologies to express themselves while bypassing many of the old obstacles. The discussion of information technology, in which I spent most of my "professional career," explores the changes in workplace economic security that would be essential to freedom. The essay on narcissism is one of the most often visited on my web domain and pins down the psychological issues of new expressive freedoms.

This book is structured as an anthology of stand-alone essays that may be read in any order. Some material may be repeated among the essays. Therefore no major attempt in editing has been made to force the essays to fit into one single-threaded argument.

As I have indicated on my hppub website, I am interested in collaborating with other writers and publishers to produce a larger work dealing with the balancing of civil liberties with national security and general welfare. Such a work should objectively examine practical, military, legal and constitutional questions involved in striking this balance in a systematic, well-organized manner, and would be a compelling item for any reader concerned about this balance. This short book stresses the areas in which I have my own targeted comments and knowledge. The issue is grave and not one that simply yields to propaganda on one side or the other.

I should mention my use of the phrase "Do Ask, Do Tell" in the title. As of this writing, no other published book that I can find starts with this title. Various web sites have mentioned it in connection with such subjects as psychological counseling, talk shows, local history, and particularly AIDS and STD prevention. It seems likely to me that the phrase would appeal to a studio as a film title. There was one attempt to trademark this phrase in the middle 1990s for use in selling memorabilia, book-promotion materials and clothing; but that attempt was abandoned. I do not believe that this phrase, because of its common use and political connotation, is appropriate for "strong" commercial branding in the sense usually required by trademark law.

In the event of a website domain-name change in the future, materials on hppub.com will be found on johnwboushka.com.

Bill Boushka
Minneapolis, MN
August 2002

1:

THE WINDING ROAD TOWARD LIBERTY

On a chilly Thanksgiving Friday in 1995, I entertained myself with a pleasant geological analogy as I drove US-29 from Arlington to Charlottesville to visit Monticello. If you map a day to five years of elapsed time, our political system was about like the East Coast in February just after a deep low forms in south Texas. You have a pretty good chance of a massive Nor'easter "perfect snowstorm" two days later. And, I thought, some kind of constitutional crisis (dwarfing Watergate) in a decade or so seemed inevitable. In a time of unusual prosperity brought about by technological change, we found ourselves squabbling about the most basic individual rights at the deepest psychological levels.

I have argued in my two previous books that the firewall between government and citizens needs to be strengthened to protect individual rights in all kinds of areas, such as the military, family values, gay issues, civil asset forfeitures, self-defense and free speech. I have suggested that some kind of constitutional amending process, perhaps a series of public town halls, would eventually become inevitable. At the same time I have proposed that moral values be cast in an extended notion of personal accountability or authentication rather than in group-based remedies. I believe that my first self-published book did stimulate a lot of debate on the more subtle areas of moral perspective and on the role of government in implementing morality, as other authors' books, particularly those on family values, became more detailed.

In September 2000 I published a monograph of putatively final set of "do ask, do tell" essays, the most important of which is a moderately deliberate explanation of how a "Bill of Rights II" (effectively proposed in Chapter 6 of *Do Ask, Do Tell* and in all of *Our Fundamental Rights*) could come about. Then a new theme for the twenty-first century was suddenly announced with the violent, tragic, even apocalyptic events of September 11, 2001.

We have a feral, viral enemy that seems diabolical enough to use the opportunities of our own technological society—particularly those related to mobility, communication and self-expression—to destroy our modern world by clandestine and asymmetric attacks from within. This particular adversary stresses religion and an intolerant "fundamentalist" mentality (denying "peaceful coexistence") that, in its nihilistic hatred first of Jews and then apparently of all of western modernism, remarkably parallels the hatred of gays (and other "groups") by "Christian" religious extremists in our own country, an observation now even conceded by our own conservative Bush administration.

Sometimes the enemy appears almost surreal, as if it had first wanted to set up a closed alien society and separate itself in Star Wars fashion on another planet. The mode of warfare seems novel to us, although it had been seen centuries before our modern state system evolved; and, for that matter, in Vietnam our country had learned that technological superiority does not always easily defeat an underground, agile guerilla opponent. Any consideration of history during the preceding decades shows a gradual accumulation of clues that this kind of new warfare was possible.

When I authored the first *Do Ask Do Tell* book and placed so much attention upon both the draft and gays in the military (and their possible future nexus) I focused much of my own thinking on the truism that individual self-expressive freedom can never be taken for granted and invokes responsibilities to participate in freedom's defense; but I saw the major threats as likely to derive from a resurgence of communism or excess nationalism in Russia or even from neo-Nazism, as in the recent film (and Tom Clancy novel), *The Sum of All Fears*. Certainly our own domestic terrorists sometimes relate to a Nazi-like world-view, which has some major psychological differences from militant Islamic radicalism.

The other major exposure to thinking about a major societal calamity for me had come with the AIDS epidemic in the 1980s. At least in the earlier days of the epidemic, the idea that the forthcoming public health catastrophe could undermine social order and civil liberties deserved serious thought. Now we see the same kind of thinking when we contemplate bio-terrorism.

So, in presenting my material, I must deal with a bifurcation. I would deal first with the principles underlying the Bill of Rights and how we should publicly review them. But then we must review all the security measures that we now need in view of the cost they may impose on civil liberties. This discussion goes beyond mechanical dissections of constitutional law. It must bring us back to thinking about what our freedom is really for and when our expectations are no longer legitimate. Frankly, we have to discuss the grim scenario of future major attacks and infrastructure breakdown, and how we would view liberty in such a world. It has happened before.

Once more, I backpeddle a bit. Over many years I noticed a trend, first with gay issues and then with most other policy problems, that "beleaguered" people—sometimes self-appointed victims—would use government to make them more comfortable in their own circumstances at the expense of the rights and freedom of others who were doing them no direct harm. This made me mad! After all, the political process, even democracy at its best, has generally dealt with people in groups defined by nationality, race, religion, age, handicapped or medical status, gender, even sexual orientation. For the most part, "groupthink" is the only kind of politics that we know.

And yet, the emergence of a technological society has given much more capability to the individual regardless of his affiliations. The last half of the twentieth century has marked an unprecedented growth in individualism for the person of average means. So it becomes natural to redirect public policy towards the notion of individual responsibility. We see increased attention to questions of what people "deserve" in terms of their own abilities and accomplishments, especially in the modern workplace.

But culturally we are very divided over the increase of individualism. After all, a philosophy of individualism, so fundamental to libertarianism, can have terrible consequences for people who "fail." Individuals can be left out in the cold even when they didn't start at the same place in line. Individualism (and the associated "market fundamentalism," as George Soros calls it, in *The Crisis of Global Capitalism*[1]) seems to contradict religious faith, to amplify social injustices or disrupt the family socialization (especially of men) that is so important both for the raising of children and the care of the elderly. Other philosophies centered on religion or communitarianism continue to be expressed. So the idea that government, through the democratic process, may force some "sacrifice" upon citizens at an individual level for the good of "all of us" still holds a lot of weight.

The experience of individualism becomes even more complicated when it confounds "family values." Since the Vietnam era we have, as a people, become increasingly divided over the importance of family and children as a primary source of personal identity—*whether one can and should be one's own person regardless of familial relationships*. And some people do not tolerate the tension over these issues well. "Gay rights" has, in psychological terms, become for some people an exercise in "tolerating" the competition and psychological distraction provided by people whose values at least *appear* to be so narcissistic, effete, aesthetic and ultimately (and paradoxically) hierarchal and exclusionary. Associated free speech has sometimes come to be viewed as a self-promoting indulgence.

After all, for so many people, family and parenting—very reproducible experiences for almost anyone willing to take a dive—do constitute "real life" and make external exercises like politics (or for that matter many kinds of conventional success) "extraneous" (let alone hedonistic). Yet to really be free, whether to experience ourselves through family or through other individual private choices, we need to shake the grip of government and special interests that find government a convenient way to gain advantage over others. We need to reduce the power of organizations that control the media and oversimplify the arguments that finally reach the people. And reducing government and reducing institutionalism itself requires a political exercise, maybe even a constitutional one.

The controversies around lesbians and gay men have become a defining test of the course of individualism. Some people on the far left want to treat gays as another minority group, with no real discussion of behavior and values. And some demagogues on the far right seem determined to re-cement the status of gays as second-class and even subservient citizens as a matter of law.

Both sides seem afraid of a real, chess-game-like sharp debate over the idea that individuals may exercise their own values in the choice of consenting significant others, and especially about the logical consequences of almost any rigid social doctrine with respect to the self-esteem of the disadvantaged. After all, some people "hide" behind their marriages, relationships, faiths, and other associations. I want to be treated exactly equal to everyone else in the law, and be able to defend my values and abilities in the free market. But traditional gay activism has sometimes seemed resigned to conceding legal inferiority (for those who can't or don't sexually practice heterosexual marriage) in some areas, especially those perceived as "social obligations" (like the military, marriage and parenting) in order to get limited discrimination and hate crimes protection ("relief") in other areas, an intellectually dishonest endeavor. The modern debates over the past ten years on gays in the military, same-sex marriage and gay parenting may indicate a real sea change. We may finally recognize that political protection of private choices alone is not enough and that equal rights and equal social responsibility may well go hand in hand.

It is possible to confuse knee-jerk "homophobia," derived directly from fear of male failure in penetrative sexual performance, with a certain philosophical viewpoint that runs underneath homophobia but remains poorly articulated. Homosexuals (particularly men) and the politicians helping them are denying the "obvious" problems with homosexual conduct and values (and deliberately hiding these problems within a dubious notion—"object"—of "immutability"). These problems include an unpredictable downstream hazard to public health, an evasion of the gender-related obligations that any civilization must demand, and a narcissistic value system that logically implies that people, once they can no longer take care of themselves or particularly "turn others on" should go out in the cold to die, like mice seeking water after eating poison.

One particularly disturbing interpretation of the "Oscar Wilde" view of homosexuality, with its emphasis on "youth," is that fantasy-like aestheticism may, if run amok, lead to an almost Nazi-like disdain or contempt for those individuals who "don't have it." All of this is stated in the subjunctive. One could make the same comments about a lot of heterosexual society, and one could rebut these points.

In fact, as a younger man I tremendously resented the automaticity of the heterosexual "family" and the way that the family seemed like a convenient cover for men who had let themselves go but who somehow expected reward for biological competence in heterosexual performance and subsequent lineage. But what bridges obligation to responsible private choice seems, to many people, to be the proper direction of sexual energy or imagination and personal motivation ("what makes you tick") into the nuclear *agape*-loving family; otherwise obligations really become burdens, life-defining sacrifices, and exercises in "paying your dues." The other big bridge, of course, would be religious faith—when construed as a humility about approaching one's own purposes in the face of "God's will" (and when perceived as a way out of confounding, labyrinthine rational debate or out of taking full responsibility for one's own troubles).

The story of the last fifty years is the gradual deregulation of the individual psyche. Increased personal responsibility must go with that, and this responsibility may well include proving that one can take care of others. The new individualism allows more expressive "private choice" including sexual choice. It demands more inflexible personal accountability and still recognizes common social obligations as spontaneously ordered "rules." New individualism also recognizes that there must be limits on the rightful prerogatives of any specific other person to tell an individual what he "owes," lest all the old corruptions of power and bureaucracy return.

The moral questions around individualism, faith, community and family still remain, however. Perhaps we will still reach a cultural understanding that every adult ought to prove that he (or she) can take care of other(s) besides himself. Ironically we will need to get government out of the way to realize this, and to help people see past the surface narcissism of some "gay values". President Bush said, when addressing Ohio State at a commencement ceremony, "A person without responsibility for others is a person who is truly alone." We must develop this understanding, if individualism is not some day to undermine our respect for life itself. Intellectuals disagree about the reach of individual understanding of cultural problems when attacking social problems with collective action. But responsible individualism implies developing this understanding and acting upon it. While freedom cannot be won or secured just by addressing the grievances of oppressed groups, neither can it be secured by a simplistic idea of individual harmlessness; freedom must deal with inequalities at the most personal levels. In order to limit the reach of government in these moral matters, we need a new debate on our constitutional rights. Senator John McCain puts things well when he says that individualism needs to find causes greater than the self.

Individualism, however, takes private choices public, because people tend to feel that their choices express who they are. That is why free speech issues have become so important to me since my original involvement with the military ban issue as an abrogation of a "privacy" right (for a servicemember or potentially conscripted civilian). The "don't ask, don't tell" policy for gays in the military now suggests that some people, like the early Christians, must publicly deny who they are in order to serve others. Therefore several of the items in this booklet (the COPA litigation discussion and the self-publishing discussion) are motivated by free speech.

And this debate must allow all arguments, including those that are politically incorrect, to be placed on the table. We must be willing to understand how others think and not run away from uncomfortable ideas by saying "I don't want to know." The threats from the outside world, as well as from some our own internal corruption, are real. We can lose it all. We must ask, and we must tell.

2:

Launching a "Bill of Rights II"

Part 1: Overview

At my hppub.com (High Productivity Publishing) website, I present a collection of writings which argue that it may be time to enhance or add to the (United States) federal Bill of Rights. In two books[2] I present my case that the firewall between people and government (federal, state and local) in several areas may need to be strengthened. Individual rights in such areas as sexual privacy, substance use, self-defense, potential conscription, free speech, religion, marriage law, freedom from discrimination because of government preferences, and freedom from inappropriate confiscation or takings of property by government all arguably might need to be strengthened.

My own libertarian approach is inductive; I rely heavily upon my experiences as a gay man particularly in dealing with the military, and then added considerable research to my own personal account. But one could live a very different life from mine and ultimately compose a narrative that comes to similar conclusions.

The libertarian paradigm for individual rights is simple. Government should interfere with an individual's choices only to the extent necessary to prohibit one individual from harming another, or to compel one individual to keep contractual promises. As a corollary, an individual is held to be absolutely responsible for himself or herself.

Of course, defining "harm" is not so simple in practice. Furthermore, a free society has to deal with community external threats (military, environmental), with pervasive social injustice inherited from the past, and with obvious inequalities among and vulnerabilities in the capabilities of individuals. Persons are called upon to make personal sacrifices to meet these needs, and these ukases rise to the level of moral imperatives. "Morals" laws, as well as forced redistribution of wealth, are seen as essential ways to make civilization fairer for vulnerable people (and not just children); democratic political process (majority rule?), balanced by separation of powers, is supposed to keep these laws fair and evenhanded. All of this fits into a notion that the courts refer to as **ordered liberty**. A paradigm based on "personal responsibility fundamentalism" (becoming more popular today as evidenced in tougher mandatory sentences for crime) may have to be tempered by the observation that many people do not have the same opportunity to execute personal choices as, say, I have had.

If these more collective concerns about the **general welfare** must drive policy, the problem is how do you draw the line in some principled way when you must encroach upon individual rights? Freedom in a gigantic pluralistic society does incur some risk; how does one determine (other than pragmatic political consensus) to what extent we will be held accountable as our brothers' keepers?

Very often, legislative attempts to draw these lines seem to express more a sense of political barter than moral thinking. One could suggest, however, that the line should be drawn when the capacity for the individual to express or actualize himself as distinct from others is materially jeopardized. One may also say that government should have the authority to tax in order to supply "basic services" (which in theory benefit all citizens equally but still provide general welfare to all individuals) but not to entrench itself politically by providing spoils for one interest group at the expense to everyone else; this (like pornography) is a difficult distinction ("a distinction with a difference") to define, but perhaps you know it when you see it.

On the other hand, when collectivism and state-forced "equality" determine what is permissible, everyone is impoverished. Freedom works; cultural communism does not. Government in a "libertarian" democracy could set out to minimize the number of people who need help rather than help people who already need help (often because of past group injustices, especially those abetted by government).

Underneath all of this lies the moral discomfort over the whole concept of "self ownership," a notion well supported by writings about "natural rights" for centuries in Western Culture.[3] Indeed, various philosophers have characterized "natural rights" as those which must exist for individuals before any government can legitimately operate. Self-ownership has become a more influential notion in the past few decades as individuals become more likely to define their own personal objectives without the prerequisite approval of others or obvious social or familial utility.

In times of great public distress over some calamity (perhaps now after 9-11), some people will talk as if they were ashamed of their own individual rights, or at least unaware that if they trade away the rights of others they are endangering their own. Even among progressive thinkers, there is a growing awareness that people need to factor properly the meeting of the real needs of others (most often through a family structure) in setting their own priorities, and that this needs to be made clear especially to young adults. One sees this kind of thinking, of course, in religion, where there is often a mistrust of the capacity for individuals to analyze moral choices on their own and in the psychological growth movement, as I noted in my discussions of the Ninth Street Center.[4] People who fail to do this may not always face legal sanction, but they find their interpersonal effectiveness compromised, especially as they grow older. No one is completely autonomous.

The paradox of our interdependence among one another in an open "advanced" society has been underscored by the calamitous terrorist attacks upon our country in late 2001. Indeed, it sometimes seems as if the attacks were intended to punish us as individuals for what we stand for, rather than just blackmail our government for its foreign policies, controversial as they may seem to some people. The underlying and shocking threat of asymmetric warfare, that it could suddenly inflict damage and casualties so massive as to make our current society unworkable for a long time, raises first the question of what kinds of liberties might be compromised in the effort to detect and prevent larger terrorist attacks, and also raises the issue of how liberty could function in a post-apocalyptic society, perhaps subject to martial law if civil authority is still in place.

To some extent, this second question has always been with us, during World War II and also the Cold War ("duck and cover"), and it poses a scenario so unacceptable as to be outside the bounds of discussion here. But prevention of attacks against the homeland, whether conventional or terroristic in nature, should be achievable without surrendering our constitutional civil liberties; national defense and security have always been factored into discussions about civil liberties in principled ways. Libertarians are correct to point out that in some cases our overly interventionist foreign policies may have future unintended consequences, inviting hatred and aggression, even when these policies seem to have succeeded at first. We do have to look at a number of issues in technical detail, and that is done in a later chapter in this book. The underlying question remains the same: balancing, with some psychological subtlety, individual freedom and self-expression with obligations to others. This balance should be the focus of future debate.

Part 2: Some Terminology and Facts about Rights

The federal Bill of Rights became law in 1791 (over 200 years ago), and in 1833 (over 160 years ago) the Supreme Court ruled that the Bill of

Rights constrained only the federal government, not the states. But with the 14th Amendment in 1865, it became possible for the Supreme Court to gradually apply ("incorporate") many provisions in the Bill of Rights to the states.

There was originally a lot of resistance to the notion of a federal Bill of Rights. It was felt that the enumeration of specific rights could imply that no other rights than those enumerated were protected. Therefore, the Bill of Rights included a 9th Amendment reserving unenumerated rights to the states and the people, and the 10th Amendment reserving unenumerated powers to the states.

In fact, many libertarians feel that the most appropriate focus of political efforts should be to confine the activities of the federal government (especially in regulation) to those powers explicitly given to it in the Constitution. Economic competition would then force states and localities to maintain a hands-off approach in their own public policies. However, state and local laws can be as oppressive as federal, and it is unlikely, given constitutional jurisprudence to date, that the 9th Amendment alone can be counted on to restrain these governments since the Courts have never really regarded it as "incorporated." Most legal scholars still regard the "penumbra" of rights in the 9th Amendment as applying specifically to limitations of federal government regulation.

The accepted term for rights very explicitly enumerated in the Constitution and its amendments is **original rights**. I used to use the term **affirmative rights** but this term has been used in other ways.[5] Another term, **fundamental rights**, is more inclusive, and this term generally refers to rights extended to protect individuals from the states as well as federal government. It refers to rights that the federal courts (and especially the Supreme Court) are willing to "derive" from existing rights and a cultural tradition concerning these rights. Fundamental rights often deal with objectives of self-expression and, therefore, self-ownership. The substantive due process clause of the 14th Amendment (applied to natural rights of "life, liberty, or property"), which generally means that laws must be "fair" to individuals, is often regarded as the source of fundamental rights, as may be other provisions, such as the 3rd Amendment (quartering of soldiers), which has been used to bolster a right to privacy, and the 5th and 9th Amendments. (Technically, the 5th Amendment had established the idea of "substantive due process" with respect to the federal government, and the 14th applied the concept—somewhat more rhetorically—to the states.) The notion of fundamental rights has been used to affirm the right to contraception and (in a limited way) abortion, but not, for example, to sodomy or drug use or, in many circumstances, concealed-carry of weapons by an individual. Generally, fundamental rights will invoke strict scrutiny from the courts; the state must show a compelling interest in compromising a fundamental right.

There is a rough correlation between the distinction separating a procedural right to privacy (from unreasonable search and seizure of private property, as guaranteed by the 4th Amendment) from **private choices** (such as sexual choice or reproductive choices), and the difference between affirmative and fundamental rights, as outlined by Amitai Etzioni in Chapter 6, "A Contemporary Conception of Privacy," *The Limits of Privacy* (1999)[6]. The notion that one has a right to a "private life" without McCarthyistic interventions from society didn't take hold until the 1890's, perhaps with a famous *Harvard Law Journal* essay "The Right to Privacy" by Bandeis and Warren.[7] (The essay was more influential in the tort system, with invasion of privacy lawsuits against publishers, authors and the press at first than it was against government; but it did instantiate the idea that privacy could be a fundamental right separate from property.)

Private choice comports with self-ownership and the setting of personal goals; yet only the first two of the Bill of Rights seem to affirm such choice as a right; the remainder of affirmative rights (or original rights) indeed have more to do with procedural protections against federal government intrusions. Indeed, "substantive due process" does not require that the fact that the public may not observe a behavior (say, bomb making or drug cultivation) means that the state may not prohibit it; the clause does not mean that government may not rebuttably presume that prohibited acts are likely to take place in some circumstances. (Here, we could analyze the comparison between the spread of computer viruses from "private" activity with the spread of real ones from sexual activity, and the reader can determine where the analogy breaks down.)

Private choices, arguably, may be tempered by their unseen collective effects on others; so traditional political theory would maintain that the checks and balances of constitutional government should prevent government prohibitions or disincentives of preferences regarding certain behaviors from becoming truly invasive (and from interfering with more subtle community and family pressures to channel individual motivation and behavior in to being able to take responsibility for others).

Another concept is **social rights**, which grow out of legislation intended to provide a safety net (such as welfare and Medicaid) and to ensure social justice, including freedom from discrimination by private institutions (discrimination by government is supposed to be prohibited by the 14th Amendment, but it took until 1954 in the *Brown* case to establish convincingly this limitation this even with respect to race). Social rights generally do not invoke constitutional questions but they do require thinking about what seems to be fair treatment by government in a civil society.

In *Our Fundamental Rights* I provided a general (not necessarily legal) discussion of the ethical framework for all of these categories of rights. Social rights may be created (by political process and consent although not by the Constitution itself), whereas fundamental rights may (conceptually speaking) only be protected and not created. Sometimes social rights can be established only by forcibly compromising the rights of some for the benefit of others whom the political process determines to be "needier."[8]

Social rights might be invoked indirectly in a libertarian society by encouraging a lifetime plan of financial responsibility. The "social rights" concept brings up, for some people, a notion of egalitarianism. A market economy (capitalism) assumes that when people act with their own resources in their own "enlightened" self-interest and produce wealth, others will gradually benefit (although, especially at first, not "equally"); the inequality (and, sometimes, personal failure) that results is not acceptable to some people and is confused with "exploitation."

A political system based on individual rights and responsibilities (and individual or private production initiatives—"self-ownership") must still grapple with questions of fairness, proper respect for the real needs of others, loyalty, and other moral notions fundamental to civil society. See also note[9] regarding a proposal by Bruce Ackerman. A "social right" to guaranteed health care (mentioned as an unquestionable right in Michael Moore's film *Bowling for Columbine*), or to freedom from unreasonable overtime in the workplace, or even to paid maternity leave, could, in the minds of some people, be derived from a affirmative or fundamental right to life. Some people will carry social rights further. For example, attempts to force welfare mothers back to work are seen as violating a right to a safety net or especially the rights of children. Such a claimed right would have to be weighed against the responsibility of the beneficiary for his or her own actions or of others connected (such as "deadbeat dads") to the person, but such conservative arguments are seen angrily by many as mean-spirited, divisive and as intended to blame victims of social injustice.

There can occur a good debate when two apparently "essential" rights come into legitimate conflict. For example, the property rights of one person or entity (inasmuch as "libertarian rights theory" treats businesses and persons equally, although a "bill of rights" would concern only individuals) may be compared to the right of an individual to be free from irrational discrimination. If property rights are fundamental and freedom from discrimination is "social," then property rights would prevail. But perhaps the right to choose a consenting adult significant other could be perceived (in a manner similar to practicing religious faith or no faith) as fundamental, too, and set up a really interesting (at least on paper) contest.

Part 3: Methods of Amending the Constitution

The Constitution (in Article V) provides two methods of amendment. It also preemptively prohibited constitutional amendment for a couple of special issues relating to slave trade (before 1808) and a state's right to representation. The Constitution has been amended 17 times since 1791, with one of the amendments (Prohibition, Amendment 18) repealed (by Amendment 21).

Method 1: Congress must pass the proposed amendment by a 2/3 majority in both House and Senate; the amendment must then be ratified by 3/4 of the states, either by state legislatures or state conventions (as specified by Congress). The state convention ratification method has been used only once, for the 21st Amendment, to repeal prohibition. Congress does have the right to stipulate a time limit for ratification, which can make ratification difficult in practice.

This method has been tried recently without success for some controversial issues, including an equal rights amendment (for women). So a constitutional amendment protecting, say, consensual sex from state legislation would have prevail in debate and a floor vote in both houses of Congress before submission to ratification. Sounds unlikely?

Method 2: An amendment(s) can be proposed by a convention called by 2/3 of the state legislatures and then be ratified by 3/4 of the state legislatures (As above, Congress could require ratifications by state conventions from 3/4of the states.)

The method has never actually been used. However, during the 1970s and 1980s, 32 states (two short of the required 34) passed resolutions calling for a constitutional convention to pass a balanced budget amendment. Some states have since retracted these resolutions, and some resolutions may have expired by now.

There is a particular controversy over this method. If such a convention took place, it is possible that any issue could be raised, and that conceivably the whole Constitution could be rewritten. Legal scholars differ on whether this is the case. However in his 1990 confirmation hearings Justice David Souter remarked that such a possibility could not be ruled out since, after all, the Constitution grew out of an intent to rewrite the Articles of Confederation. Another controversy is the idea that citizens of a state might be able to substitute themselves for the state legislature and propose a convention by referendum.

Were enough of the 32 resolutions (for the balanced budget amendment) still active and were some states to propose a convention over some other issue (perhaps even abortion), then a pressure group or even a private citizen conceivably (theoretically) could take legal action to force a convention, which according to some theorists could be forced to address any issue. Were this to happen, the instance could appear quite suddenly and throw financial markets and political institutions into chaos. Earlier during my adulthood, I would often hear left-wing groups like "The People's Party" throw around talk of forcing another constitutional convention as if it were as easy as the "second Russian revolution" of 1991.

There is one advantage to the "runaway convention," however. Since one issue alone would probably not be presented, we would not have the problem of debating an emotional issue (like abortion) out of context, out of principled relationships to other issues. A few scholars (Charles Black at Yale in the 1960s) have argued that Article V (as interpreted historically and textually) would allow only "unlimited" conventions (Article V reads verbatim, "shall call a convention for proposing amendments"), but most mainstream legal observers believe that the Constitutional Convention Implementation Act of 1991 (or at least the powers designated to Congress and the states) makes a "revolutionary convention" as opposed to a "limited" convention unlikely. (But may the Congress or may the states themselves "interpret" Article V, or is this up to the judiciary? See Vile in note 8 above.)

There is not a lot written on this convention method, but my site (hppub.com) will present more material as it finds it. Some sources are listed below.[10] See the list of states that have called for a constitutional convention (current as of 1994) at (hppub.com/states.htm). The "threat" of the convention method is more one of psychological subterfuge; conservatives could assemble some hot-button issues (like abortion, school religious displays or prayer, flag burning or guns) into a package and over a period of time surreptitiously lobby states (starting with those who called for the balanced budget amendment) into authorizing a convention without forcing a roll call vote in Congress—if they thought they had a warrant, let's say, from a right-to-life president and Congress. The end result of such a convention could be the cultural interpretation process in my next section.[11] Or perhaps pressure to pass a specific amendment proposal (like the balanced budget or, as desired by 2000 Republican presidential candidate George W. Bush, overturning *Roe v. Wade*) by the "safer" first method in Congress. In May 2002 Rep. Bob Barr from Florida (Rep), with the backing of the socially conservative Alliance for Marriage, introduced a Federal Marriage Amendment (FMA) in the House of Representatives that limited the only acceptable definition of marriage to be between a male and female. It is unclear to me whether this would apply only at the federal level or whether it would wipe out all domestic partnership laws in benefits passed by states and local governments. See my "Amendment 29" in Chapter 6 of *Do Ask, Do Tell.*

The text of the FMA amendment reads: "Marriage in the United States shall consist only of the union of a man and a woman. Neither this constitution or the constitution of any state, nor state or federal law, shall be construed to require that marital status or the legal incidents thereof be conferred upon unmarried couples or groups." Other specific scenarios that could conceivably attract interest in constitutional amendment include reparations for slavery, and a victim's rights amendment.

Part 4: Changing the Cultural Interpretation of the Bill of Rights (a "Virtual" Bill of Rights II)

But there is still another way!

There may exist an opportunity to mediate the way the courts view the extraction of new "fundamental rights" from already established rights. This notion has to do with the controversy over "original intent," "interpretivism" and "textualism," as represented by the opposing points of view of Justice Anthony Scalia on the one hand and liberal Harvard law professor Lawrence Tribe on the other. Morton Kaplan (normally perceived as a social conservative) recently covered this controversy with an excellent essay[12] in which he outlines the proper middle ground in interpreting the notion of fundamental right (particularly as associated with the [substantive] due process clause of the 14th Amendment and "life, liberty, or property" interests) in the "modern" world.[13]

For example, "original meaning, even if already known, should not prevail over durably changed culture; and judicial recognition of change ought not to occur until it is durable change, especially in the face of evidence to the contrary." Mr. Kaplan's ideas would not apply to the "creation" of social rights or entitlements, which are generally accomplished legislatively or through political process.

Essentially, it may be proper to extract a new fundamental right when there is ample evidence that the social culture has already evolved to the point that most people believe that they have this putative right. It is essential that the social thought has already "changed" and is not merely still "changing." In some way, Mr. Kaplan's theory comports with the British idea of an informal, organic constitution as a growing collection of public documents taking positions on critical political process and scope issues. Still, from a conservative this is somewhat a novel idea, especially when one considers that originally the founding fathers did not envision a populist democracy, but rather a republic that somewhat benefited property owners.

Actually, we have seen this process of appealing to public tradition already in various cases (*Griswold, Roe v. Wade,* and [as failed] *Bowers v. Hardwick*). In these cases the Court has tried to establish and then bound a fundamental right to privacy (at least a limited fundamental right). But in *Hardwick,* the Court majority refused to accept that there was such a thing as a "fundamental right to engage in homosexual sodomy."[14] Tradition (the kind that Dr. Robert Schuler talks about in his "Hour of Power") only fully protects sexual activity when it is somehow (even loosely) connected to marriage, family, and possible procreation (and complementarity). Justice Burger reinforced this notion with a tirade about how antipathy towards homosexuality has "ancient roots."

Apparently, in the mind of the Court in 1986, individual rights assume more legitimacy when exercised in the context of the traditional family or in some sort of "altruistic" activity than when carried out by a person simply serving his own immediate ends. This point will be an important overriding concern in some of the questions below.

A good conceptual example of a fundamental right extracted from existing rights is the "right to travel" (between states), which the Supreme Court has held to be understood as a fundamental right from the principles of federalism. This right has been used to strike down laws limiting state welfare benefits to newly arrived residents (from states with lower benefits).

Is there a systematic way to establish and document that a change in public attitude has actually occurred?

My proposal would be to take up Ross Perot on his suggestion in the 1992 presidential campaign, that there be staged a series of national "town meetings"—a minimum of four, in different cities (I like starting in Williamsburg)—to draw up a consensus document on individual fundamental rights. Such a document would have to document in great detail evidence for its positions. This evidence could consist of a lot of sources, such as published materials (I guess my own effort to document this in *Do Ask, Do Tell* counts in the numbers) and the record of how various disputes may have been settled outside of the court system (such as conflict of interest problems in the workplace). It would not be directly legally binding, but it would help provide the cultural evidence that the courts need in interpreting text in the context of changed culture. It would provide a bridge between "accepted" moral or ethical culture (particularly with respect to motivational and values issues) and actual common law.

In *Do Ask, Do Tell*, I provided some historical documentation of a process like this, called "The Area of Mutual Agreement," as was attempted in the late 1970s.[15] This debate, which will structure basic moral values and map government's relationships to these values, is fundamentally different from the traditionally liberal democratic political process in that moral values are not taken simultaneously by "fuzzy logic" both as an irreducible given and as the product of majoritarian political barter. This approach tends to become intolerant of individual moral or scientific inquiry if it gets in the way of the apparently necessarily adversarial political coalitions.

But the development of "shadow conventions" (to tag along the Republican and Democratic 2000 conventions in Philadephia and Los Angeles respectively) were a good start. Arianna Huffington described these on ABC's "Good Morning America" on July 28, 2000. The Philadelphia convention featured Jesse Jackson and John McCain as speakers and dealt with issues such as campaign finance reform, the war on drugs (and whether it targets African-Americans), and the presence of so much child poverty in a booming economy—all of these practical rather than constitutional questions, yet they could anchor the kind of consensus that Kaplan is talking about.

It is worth noting that at the state constitutional level, the recognition of "fundamental rights" is sometimes stronger and more encompassing and not so dependent on "traditionalism" as perhaps it is at the federal level. See Selland.[16]

Part 5: Questions for a Town-Hall Convention

Questions that have potential immediate constitutional significance are marked with an asterisk (*). I am trying to focus on the aspects of the debate that don't usually get enough deliberate attention.

General Questions

(A1) Can individuals derive principles of ethical or moral behavior without blindly following religious precepts or authority?

(A2)* Is it ever acceptable for the state to suspend civil liberties (affirmative and fundamental rights) in a time of dire national emergency (as with declaring martial law) from external environmental, public health, military threats, or internal terrorist threats? For example, may persons be held without formal charge as "unlawful combatants?" May the 4th Amendment prohibition against unreasonable search and seizure be abrogated for special eavesdropping to intercept weapons of mass destruction?

(A3) Libertarians maintain that everyone should be able to keep everything he or she earns. The left will claim that no one earns all that he has, that everyone depends upon a social infrastructure and this must be fair. Is the redistribution of wealth or opportunity to rectify unfairness an appropriate function of democratic government? [17]

(A4) Should the state be allowed to suspend a certain civil liberty because of the inability of some people to control themselves when everyone has that liberty?

(A5) Assume an "enlightened" legislature (representing a well-publicly-educated and vigilant electorate) is trying to weigh whether the following individual rights should be protected from intrusion by society's collective concerns: (A5.1) A man living in the inner city wants to own a machine gun to defend his large family. (A5.2) A homosexual wants to choose a same-sex marriage partner or sexual partner without interference from the state and without discrimination. (A5.3) A small business-man owning a small publishing company wants to present moderately adult gay materials at his internet site to attract traffic. (A5.4) Another web operator wants to offer bomb-making instructions at his site. (A5.5) A duplex homeowner does not want to rent the other apartment to a same-sex couple because of his personal religious convictions. By what principles does the legislature decide when someone's fundamental rights are abridged or when society's interest in "general welfare" or equality overrides this objection?

(A6) Should the law (positive or common) be the only repository of societal judgments about right and wrong? Should some moral notions be left for people to decide on their own?

(A7) What constitutional principles should limit the application of the incorporation doctrine?

(A8) Should states enjoy sovereign immunity, particularly with respect to lawsuits demanding monetary damages for discrimination in violation of the 14th Amendment or federal law?

(A9) Should the Constitution limit the acts which federal government may regard as crimes (in accordance with the 9th and 10th Amendments)? Some scholars maintain that the federal government is authorized to criminalize only treason, counterfeiting, and piracy; all other criminal wrongs are to be left to states and local governments.

(A10) May government, through a democratic process, rightfully force citizens to compromise their private expressive choices as an indirect result of implementing common good?

(A11) Would the "double jeopardy" clause of the 5th Amendment prevent two different prosecutions against different defendants for the same crime for different theories of guilt (the *King* case in Pensacola, Fl., 2002)?

(A12) Will America be able to maintain an open society with practical civil liberties and self-ownership if an enemy through asymmetric warfare is sufficiently determined to force our society to implement in our legal system its religious or moralistic vision?

(A13) Are there any circumstances during the war on terror when *Posse Comitatus* (1878) should be overruled in the course of homeland defense?

Preferences and Discrimination

(B1)* Does a legal mandate prohibiting discrimination against members of a perceived class mean that affirmative steps must be taken to benefit this class at the expense to persons not in the class? Examine in the context of the 14th Amendment.

(B2) Are burdens on families with children so great that affirmative steps must be taken that would result in persons without dependents being forced to help support them to an extent much greater than today?

(B3) Do laws prohibiting discrimination improperly intrude upon property rights?

(B4) If the state should prohibit discrimination, should it treat individuals, small businesses and large organizations, as possible agents of discrimination, differently?

(B5) Does one have a fundamental right not to be the "victim" of reverse discrimination because of a retroactively corrective advantage given to a class?

(B6) Should some discrimination categories (age, disability, even sexual orientation) be left to the states to regulate (and left alone by the federal government)? Is the "libertarian paradigm" more appropriate for some categories than for others (like race)? May states discriminate on the basis, say, of age or disability even though the federal government may not? What does the 14th Amendment mean when it refers to "any person?"

(B7) Suppose a government entity passes a law requiring employers to pay a "family wage"—that is, to pay married people with children more than others, or to protect such persons from layoff. Or suppose the entity passes a law forbidding this. Would either of these measures be constitutional? Should they be? Is this kind of judgment the proper use of the "democratic" political process?

(B8) Suppose that evidence that fossil fuels contribute to global warming really does become convincing and Congress or a state wants to pass a law allowing people to drive gasoline-powered vehicles only when there are two or more occupants in a car, or only on certain days of the week, possibly considering a person's family status or having dependents. Would this be constitutional? Should it be? Is it an appropriate use of democratic political process?

Right to Life/Right to Die

(C1)* The debate on when human life begins is familiar. One can be glib and say that a mother who does not want to protect unborn life from conception need not have engaged in sexual intercourse to begin with. But does the obligation to protect human life mean that all arguably human life must be protected regardless of the personal cost to others? This is more of an issue with an aging population.

(C2)* Do prospective parents have the right to manipulate the genes of the child that they intend to bear, in order to have the perfect son or daughter ("My Boy Bill" from the show *Carousel*)?[18]

Sexual Privacy

(D1)* Is it improper for a state to pass a law (like a sodomy law) that it knows has little chance of direct enforcement but that sets up a "rebuttable presumption" situation that the state can then use for discrimination (as in gay adoption or child custody cases)? Should this now be understood to violate substantive due process?

(D2)* Do public health concerns (HIV or future undiscovered viruses) justify state prohibition against certain sexual practices?

(D3)* To what extent does commercial intent (prostitution) undermine a claim of sexual privacy if it otherwise is found to exist?

(D4)* To what extent are members of the military entitled to sexual privacy (from members of the opposite sex and even from homosexuals)?

(D5)* Does a "what if everybody did it?" argument apply to a debate about a fundamental right to private adult homosexual conduct?

(D6) Should we establish a fundamental right to choice of consenting adult partner(s)? If we did, would there be a fundamental right of any two competent adults to marry and have legal recognition (including certain privileges) for their relationship, particularly if established as a covenant? What about a right for a man to cohabit with more than one female partner (and let's even assume that the law recognizes only the first marriage, or that the man divorces before each additional marriage)? Ref: CBS "48 Hours" story on polygamy, Nov. 18, 1999.

(D7) Is it reasonable to presume that sodomy refers particularly to certain male homosexual behavior (and not to certain behaviors in opposite-sex intimacies?)

Drugs and Substance Abuse

(E1)* Why is it necessary to deny cancer and AIDS patients medical marijuana? (Consider that such patients may have difficulty taking oral medications.)

(E2)* Are controlled substances harmful to everyone who uses them or only to some people? Should a behavior be illegal for everyone if only some people are predisposed to harm from it?

(E3)* Would a right to privacy apply to drug use in the way it applies (if it indeed does) to consensual sexual behavior?

(E4) Would crime rates go down if we eliminated the war on drugs? What would happen with actual drug abuse?

(E5) May the government prosecute or penalize citizens for drug activity discovered in unrelated government operations (such as HUD inspections of apartment residences)?

Guns

(F1) Who is liable for a crime committed with a weapon? The person who commits the crime? The person who unknowingly makes the weapons available? The manufacturers of weapons?

(F2)* Is self-defense partly a personal responsibility (for the head of a family), or should it belong entirely to recognized law enforcement?

(F3)* Was the 2nd Amendment intended as an individual right or only to protect the rights of states and localities to have their own militias?

(F4)* Is the possibility of oppressive government or ineffective law enforcement legally a justification for gun ownership? Is the idea that government might have to be overthrown in a revolutionary movement a valid justification for the right to bear arms?

(F5)* Should property owners be allowed to use deadly force or retaliatory devices (such as man-traps) to protect their property when life itself is not in jeopardy?

(F6)* May government constitutionally determine that there are certain weapons of a size or destructiveness that no individual should be able to obtain or own them, even in the privacy of his own home?

(F7)* Does the phrase "a well-regulated militia" in the 2nd Amendment imply (according to the changed culture idea mentioned above) that weapons ownership for self-defense is an affirmative right only when exercised with some degree of community supervision?

(F8) Suppose a legislature limits the number of guns a person can buy to one a month, to hinder "parking lot car trunk" sales. Is this a reasonable and legitimate limitation on gun ownership for public safety?

(F9) Would gun fingerprinting comply with due process requirements?

Free Speech, Freedom of Religion, and other First Amendment Issues

(G1)* Is there a principled way in which society can draw the line in prohibiting certain materials (sexually explicit or weapons related) from being available to children or mentally unstable people through the Internet? What is the least restrictive means" available to protect minors from harmful materials? Similar questions can be posed about other media (print, magazines, movies and especially, in the light of the Littleton, Colorado tragedy, video games). To play devils's advocate, visit the selected court testimony on the "Hitman" case at the hppub.com site (file hitman.htm). Could very violent speech be regarded as "obscenity"? (hppub.com/hitman.htm).

(G2)* Do commercial enterprises (including individual self-publishers) have the same free speech rights as individuals engaging in personal speech? If the answer is (sometimes) "no," then does the size or corporate structure or non-profit status of the entity affect the result? (Consider the example set by the fair use provision of federal copyright law.) Consider, however, freedom of the press (many presses are commercial and this site is arguably a press); consider free speech limitations of advertising and whether Internet teasers and free content amount to advertising. See also the June 1999 casino ruling on commercial advertising at hppub.com/chrono.htm. Does a formal established press sometimes have stronger free speech rights than an individual speaker with commercial motives?

(G3) Is self-publishing (the "village-square soap box") an effective and legitimate way to influence debate? Or does it tend to unfairly drag others in? Some commentators have called (extremist) Internet self-publishing a tactic of wimps!

(G4) Is the absence of supervision for self-publishing (especially on the Internet) a public safety concern? If so, wouldn't bureaucratic review hinder legitimate free speech?

(G5)* Do non-verbal acts of defiance such as flag-burning or draft-card burning constitute legitimate free speech? Is flag-burning essentially a form of cultural obscenity?

(G6)* If private consensual sodomy may be made illegal, may speech (such as on public areas of the Internet) which encourages such behavior be made illegal? Or would this be an unconstitutional form of circularity? What if the behavior is "especially egregious" (murder, terrorism) to "reasonable people"?

(G7)* Should the 1st Amendment protect religious organizations from laws against employment discrimination or sexual harassment? If so, does this amount to government preference for religious activity?

(G8)* Do public-property displays of religion-associated art (nativity scenes) really violate separation of church and state?

(G9)* The Supreme Court has ruled that freedom of association (though not explicitly mentioned) is a fundamental right because political action is usually more effective when carried out by groups than by individuals alone. (Hence the restrictions against employment loyalty oaths, for example.) What about the converse? Is group-sponsored speech sometimes better protected by the 1st Amendment than individual speech? Or does group-speech tend to stamp out dissenting individual speech and therefore somehow need to be regulated when it is "harmful to minorities"?

(G10)* In American law, truth is a defense to libel (ever since the colonial Peter Zenger trial). Is this of constitutional significance?

(G11)* Regarding freedom of the press, is the Internet part of the press? Will "The Fifth Estate" gain control of dissemination of information and (as Dick Morris said on "Larry King Live") precipitate a more direct democracy?

(G12)* Some groups resisting mandatory student fees at state universities for extracurricular activities are claiming a fundamental right to "not speak," that is not to be forced to contribute to airing a point of view with which one has a "moral objection." Discuss.

(G13) Is "freedom of (expressive) association" not guaranteed for operators of public accommodations? Consider *James Dale v. Boy Scouts* (1999). What about those run by religious groups? Is safe-place a legitimate expressive association concern?[19] May membership groups with a high-leve" expressive idea ever be regarded as public accommodations?

(G14) Should social association come under the 1st Amendment penumbra? (It doesn't now, because of a 1989 Supreme Court decision.) Do gay meeting places (such as bars or coffee shops) need constitutional protection of freedom of association?

(G15) Should government be able to pass laws protecting groups from offensive public speech? By race? Sexual orientation? Religion? How far should the law go in preventing bad mannered speech?

(G16) Is speech more "protected" if it is from an elected official?

(G17) Do persons who self-publish on the Internet belong to the press for the purposes of freedom of the press?

(G18) Should those in publicly owned spaces (including schools) be compelled to listen to the religious prayers of others? What about a moment of silence?

Education

(H1)* Is federal government going beyond its constitutionally-delegated powers in establishing "Profiles in Learning" and "School to Work" (as under implementation in Minnesota)?

(H2)* Should parents or students be forced to pay (through school taxes or public university tuition) for politically charged, religious (such as creation science) or sexually explicit curricula that they find objectionable?

Commerce ('I' was deliberately omitted)

(J1) How do we know when a zoning or licensing regulation of business achieves a legitimate consumer protection aim and when it instead simply protects an existing economic interest (or labor union)?

(J2) May some kinds of commerce (gambling, weapons sales) be prohibited on the Internet but allowed elsewhere?

(J3) Should there be a "free market" in transplantable organs?

(J4) Should women be allowed to carry babies for hire?

(J5) What power is implied in the Constitution by the commerce clause or similar clauses to prohibit discrimination?

(J6) To what extent must small, entrepreneurial business owners without a lot of capital for infrastructure protect the public from criminal or wantonly negligent misuse of their products or properties? Examples: owners of moderately adult web sites, small ISPs whose servers could be hijacked as zombies for denial-of- service attacks?

(J7) What powers does the commerce clause give to federal government to limit what it perceives as unfair competition?

Military

(K1)* Should the federal government continue to have the contingent power to conscript? If so, should this power still apply to men only? What about a future draft and gays in the military (don't ask, don't tell)? Could this set gays up for future Cold-War-style government-sponsored discrimination?

(K2)* Do servicemembers have a constitutional right to a zone of privacy when they are stateside, off-duty and off-base, and out-of-sight from their unit mates?

Civil Asset Forfeiture

(L1)* Does it violate the due process clause of the 14th Amendment for government to seize property and be able to keep it without gaining conviction for a crime? Is the "preponderance of the evidence" standard in civil trials fundamentally unfair if the government is the plaintiff and is using civil forfeiture as a way around the higher standard of proof required for criminal prosecution? (Examples: drug-related seizures, obscenity seizures.)

Gambling

(M1)* Why should gambling be permissible on sovereign native-American lands but not elsewhere, in many states?

(M2)* Is the fact that some adults have difficulty with compulsive gambling a good reason to regulate it for everybody?

Other

(N1) Should juries have the right to "jury nullification" of laws that they find offensive?

(N2) Should the penalty for a crime depend upon the identity of the victim as in hate crimes legislation?

(N3) Does a "don't ask, don't tell" approach (whether by the military or by organizations such as the Boy Scouts) really respect personal privacy?

(N4) Should the age of adulthood be consistent across issues? (Examples: drinking, military service eligibility, contract signing, accountability for crimes as an adult.)

(N5) Do victims of crimes need more constitutional protection in the criminal justice process? Examples: right to a court-appointed lawyer, right to speed up the trial, right to intervene in plea bargain or the decision to try a juvenile as an adult. There are arguments against this kind of proposal. See http://www.aclu.org/action/vra106.html

(N6) To what extent do immigrants here (in the United States) illegally enjoy constitutional protections? Does the libertarian proposal of completely open immigration encourage egalitarianism (or at least equal opportunity)?

(N7) Does civil psychiatric commitment violate due process? (Look at what is done to some gay teens by religious parents.) May sex offenders be incarcerated for treatment indefinitely after completing their sentences?

(N8) Suppose the eldercare and nursing home crisis worsens and Congress passes a law requiring that any unmarried adult child with assets but without other dependents stop working and care personally for an aging parent or live in the same residence. Perhaps the law could be couched in terms of eligibility of the parent's care for Medicare or Medicaid reimbursement. Here would be a case of infringement upon the rights of some supposedly privileged individuals for social good (for "family values")? Would this be constitutional? Compare to the involuntary servitude problems with conscription (and look at *Rostker v.*

Goldberg, 1981). Would filial responsibility laws (laws in previous generations that held adult children responsible for economically dependent
parents such as those in nursing homes) be constitutional if they considered marital status? Include same-sex marriage in the discussion. See section C above.

(N9) If government can no longer be involved in mediating private
choices, just what are the powers of government under checks and balances in a democracy? Which of the explicit powers in the Constitution
really require informed consensus of the people?

(N10) Suppose, in the attempt to provide health care, government passes
a law requiring that anyone who employs an outside consultant for more
than three months in order to outsource work must pay health insurance
premiums for that consultant. Or suppose that a local government
requires that anyone with a home based business must rent commercial
office space. Would these measures be constitutional?

(N11) Should juries have the right do decide that a law is unfair (according to the due process clause) or that it does not apply? This is the jury
nullification problem.

Conclusion

As a closing remark, I want to note how important the principle of personal accountability is to me as a gay man. Let me reiterate: society should
principally hold people responsible for their own personal (and visibly or
directly harmful and aggressive) actions, and not do too much else. I am
not confident of how gay men and lesbians will fare, in the long run, if
permissible conduct is determined first by the general welfare (as is definitely the case with drugs, some other "vices" and perhaps gun control) or
by a vaguely construed common good.

A behavior is, on its face, either permissible or not permissible. What
traditional activism has done is to partially concede that, perhaps, homosexuality has a questionable effect on the larger society but that, for some

people (ideally in this rhetoric a "protected class") it must be permitted or even celebrated because gay people are in some indeterminate way essentially and immutably different. At best, this presents homosexuality as a disability, an insulting idea. I want no part of it.

The proper debate (*Hardwick* notwithstanding) is not about whether gay people are a distinctly vulnerable group but about whether the choice of an adult intimate partner should be regarded as a fundamental right. A private choice of a same-sex partner, while carried out in private under reasonable expectations of privacy, putatively has indirect public effects—perhaps public health and competitive imbalance, but more relevantly, the pervasiveness of knowledge of a person's choice, the values behind that choice, what that communicates to others and how it might impact the self-image of others. So "gay rights" in the "do ask do tell" age, migrates from a privacy issue more to a free speech one, which understandably concerns some segments of society, most of all the military.

So, I personally would frame the whole discussion of a Bill of Rights II around these assertions:

(1) A definite line must be drawn to prevent government from encroaching upon the fundamental rights of its citizens. It may well be the case that the constitutional protections of individual rights should be improved.

(2) Individual rights (especially private choices) should be tied to personal accountability and responsibility. There indeed exist controversial areas of moral debate on social justice, "initial place in line," "deservedness," social obligations and the setting of personal priorities (family values). Some of these may have a bearing on affirmative rights like the right to life. But it may be better to resolve these in private, voluntary arrangements than through the force of the state (even in a democracy, even given "checks and balances"). The notion of a "bill of responsibilities"—that one should show that one can take care of others besides oneself and fulfill generic social obligations (community service) comes into consideration,

as do the informal mechanisms that assess when individuals have paid their dues without corrupting the system. (Competition among volunteer organizations is part of the answer.) Positive law comes into play when the moral case (in terms of the individual rights v. responsibilities paradigm) for a proposed public policy is overwhelming and the debate is essentially non-political.

(3) Full and open discussion is essential. It has to be possible to put practically all ideas on the table, for the record. People should understand that there is a difference between moral choices as they are generally expressed in the law (including case law) today and how they should be expressed in our culture in the future. People should understand how others think. Determining who has standing to be heard may become an interesting derivative issue.

Orlando Patterson weighs in on point 3 when he writes that liberalism evokes "moral neutralism, the idea that liberty is exclusively about the rules of right conduct and is scrupulously neutral about what is good.... The idea that people can continue truly to believe in their beliefs without believing them to be true may make sense to academics and philosophers, but for most people—contrary to Nagel's optimistic wish—it amounts to skepticism, if not cynicism."[20] Indeed, we must learn to live with the paradoxes involved in political moral neutrality; the 1st Amendment, especially freedom of religion and separation of church and state (however imperfect in practice) demands it. The political process cannot create what is good; it can mainly ratify what the majority wants and perhaps believes (however wrongly) to be good.

I can recapitulate a bit more with a certain emphasis on gay issues. "Gay activism" is accustomed to conventional political workings, where change occurs only through collective ("democratic") action. Libertarians like me have been critical of almost all conventionally collective political establishments as being morally "unprincipled." (Two wrongs don't make a right!) One could conjecture, however, that introspective moral development should occur in personal lives and be discussed in scenarios like

Laura Schlessinger talk shows (before she became "Dr. Laura" and started her name-calling), Ninth Street Center psychological discussion groups, or Minnesota PrideAlive café chats—but not in public policy debate or in the voting booth.

If self-ownership really should be circumscribed by moral and social obligations (particularly by observing "family first" values) to meet the needs of others, then what principle (besides immutability) still allows choice of an intimate partner to become a proposed fundamental right? Perhaps the psychological principle is that one does not really learn well without focusing somewhat on others, and this is very possible within gay and lesbian relationships. The political principle still is that we ought to protect individual rights and choices as much as possible while maintaining a stable, ordered liberty. It does seem to me that if society could wake up and willingly allow gays and lesbians (by choice or not) to assume social obligations (like marriage, parenting, and "half-open" (to borrow from chess opening theory military service), then collective solutions to basic questions of social justice could be proposed with much less partisanship and political adversarialism.

At the same time, we must recognize that a society that maximizes individual personal choices faces some risks, as in health care where older persons without sufficient savings and without individually competitive job skills may well literally face shortened life spans.

"Extermism in defense of liberty is no vice, and moderation in defense of liberty is no virtue." Barry Goldwater (1964) ("...you have to shoot straight" [1993]). Liberty is the "one true thing" that you have to protect for others in order to secure it for yourself.

"Bill of Rights II" has also been called "Bill of Rights 2."

3:

TERRORISM, INDIVIDUALISM, CIVIL LIBERTIES, AND LIBERTARIANISM: A PERSPECTIVE

(CAN WE STILL TALK ABOUT A "BILL OF RIGHTS II"?)

In my 1997 book *Do Ask, Do Tell*, I presented an optimistic future in which the firewall between government and the personal lives and expressions of citizens could be strengthened, possibly by augmenting the Bill of Rights. Much of my argument was based on expanding notions of personal responsibility. The libertarian notion of spontaneous order is that a gradually better-educated public will take an interest in understanding how different kinds of people think.

I also traced historically how, since the end of World War II, American (and, to a large extent, western European) society has become culturally individualistic. Younger people growing up in average economic circumstances now perceive futures in which they may define their own personal expressive agendas without the limitations of class or family—and discrimination—commonplace in the past. Ironically—and this is critical—this form of expressive individualism (as opposed to "survivalism," "frontierism" or a Luddite attitude) depends upon the interdependencies within a civilization that can make its security vulnerable. These interdependencies work only in an open society governed democratically under the **rule of law**, in a non-secular fashion, without dependence on a particular theology. And this form of law depends on a reasonable separation of church and state.

Early in my last *DADT* chapter I posed the question, "Is it safe?" I was concerned with threats to freedom, all right. I had proposed a paradigm where individualism is authenticated when every person can account for his own acts. But freedom for our culture as a whole had global, collective threats. Even then I saw epidemics, global warming, asteroids and maybe even extraterrestrials (don't expect them to be as gentle as gifted teenager Clark Kent—Clive Barker's Pie'oh'pah is more typical) as conceivable threats.

More seriously, and closer to terra, I suspected military threats from Iraq or Iran, North Korea, China, and a collapse of Russia back towards communism or super-nationalism. I knew about Osama bin Laden but saw him as only one of many threats, a minor one at that, and I was wrong there. But I was concerned about how one rebuilds a set of principles and firewalls to contain individual freedoms in view of the inevitable threats— moral and external—that would some day come. Freedom could be taken away by external agents despite our best response, or it could be taken away in misguided attempts to protect ourselves. Either scenario was viewed as possible.

Now, as of September 11, 2001, we are at war. And war ultimately threatens the ability of law and an open society to co-exist.

The nature of this new asymmetric war is particularly chilling. The empowerment of the individual, of the small company, business or organization has its flip side. To some extent this observation depends upon a certain paradox: as just noted, expressive individualism works in an interconnected society, dependent on an elaborate, open—and vulnerable—physical and informational infrastructure.

In an interconnected society, individuals may incur tremendous personal losses because of the failures of others (an observation that has underpinned the Luddite movement in the past, to the point of violence, as in the domestic Unabomber case). Individuals and persons working in small autonomous groups may do tremendous, almost apocalyptic, harm as well as innovative good. We leave portals open to an enemy that seems like the social studies equivalent of the HIV virus, a mechanism that feeds upon the very facilities that make society free, open, and productive.

Expressive freedom becomes meaningless in a society that doesn't have reasonable stability and security—although this statement is itself subject to elaboration later. Collective self-defense against any major enemy is a prerequisite for freedom. So society as a whole has to learn the social, political and especially legal equivalent of "safer sex," by psychological analogy to the gay male community's challenge starting twenty years ago (and continuing today). Having written what I have over five years (with the follow-up in *Our Fundamental Rights, Bill of Rights 2,* and my hppub.com website), I need to provide some discussion of how to balance civil liberties with very serious concerns about public safety. Of course, it is textbook social studies to say that terrorism, as a political strategy, generally aims at forcing the government of the attacked society to repress its own citizens and curtail civil liberties. In some sense citizens therefore "share the suffering" and shed their "tainted fruits" regardless of their own individual best intentions. Terrorism is very much predicated on the idea that the world is a zero-sum game. It denies the importance of individual self-direction and conceives only of group or collective agendas, whether in terms of religion, nationality, or some other cultural idea.

America—and for that matter, western Europe—now faces a greater threat on the homeland that it has at any time since the Cuban Missile Crisis of 1962. I witnessed that historical episode at the age of nineteen from the uncertain shelter of a mental health ward in the National

Institutes of Health. This near-Armageddon, which I could not have survived, became the subject of the New Line Cinema film *13 Days* in 2000. More civilians were killed in the Sept. 11 attacks on our own soil than soldiers who died in any Civil War battle, and it is likely that the War on Terrorism will claim more American civilians than military. Enormous disruptions to our way of life are possible. Freedom and economic prosperity could be on hold for a generation. In the most extreme circumstances these disruptions could conceivably bring down the United States government itself.

SEPTEMBER 11, 2001

Yup, this day has that "before and after" quality invented by Randy Shilts when writing about the sudden onset of the AIDS epidemic in *And the Band Played On.*

I had dreamed intensely all night long, and got up around 7 AM Minneapolis (Central, one hour behind New York) time. I worked a bit on my domain while watching ABC "Good Morning America" and enjoyed Cheerios. I turned off the idiot box around 7:40 A.M. intending to walk a mere 1000 feet of Skyway to work. I did a little more maintenance on my computer and around 7:50 left the apartment.

I logged on to my work computer and took care of a couple of small production support problems. Around 8:25, a young woman with whom I normally do not work appeared in my cubicle. She announced that the World Trade Center had been hit by a large plane, and then clarified that both towers had been struck as if they were pedestrians. I tried to log onto Yahoo and CNN and found the Internet clogged. I rode downstairs to the operations center where there was a Jumbotron logged on to CNN and heard that the Pentagon had just been attacked. Even the president had thought that the first plane strike had been accidental but videos of the strike slow very clearly even from Manhattan street level a wide-body commercial jet that could not have crashed unintentionally into a sky-scraper.

We were planning a workplace team outing on the Minnesota River that day—which we held anyway—but I quickly walked back to my apartment in the Churchill and tuned in to ABC. I saw Peter Jennings with the burning, enormous Twin Towers in the background. In maybe three more minutes I saw the South Tower simply disappear in a plume of smoke and ash, even before Jennings knew that it had collapsed.

I could not peek through the smoke to see the tower structure itself col-lapse from this view, but later videos on ABC would show the South Tower almost toppling (since it was struck rather lower) with the top thirty floors diving like a kid's block into smoke before the whole build-ing pancaked to the ground. The North Tower would implode in a per-fect, almost aesthetic symmetry. The antenna tower plunged straight down as the debris cloud unpeeled off tentacles before forming a huge dust devil or tornado after the collapse was completed. Later amateur videos would capture the sounds just like enormous dumpsters closing. On the outing we had no further access to information until late after-noon, and we wondered how the hijackings could even have been possi-ble.

In late October I would visit both Arlington, where I grew up, and New York. I would see the Pentagon devastation on the day of the Marine Corps marathon and spend two hours walking clockwise around the dev-astation in lower Manhattan. I would pass 100 Church Street, where in 1978 I had worked on a Medicaid project for Bradford, one of the most successful episodes in my whole I.T. career. This building was cordoned off but undamaged. Soon I would pass sidewalk vendors in masks and view the surreal, almost Strangelove destruction, which became increas-ingly visible from the south side as I approached Battery Park. Afterwards, my clothes and skin would stink with the odor of adsorbed hydrogen sul-fide from the jet fuel fumes that still raged in the "bathtub."

I would also walk around the Capitol area and see the police line tapes around House and Senate office buildings from the anthrax scare. The Supreme Court building was being evacuated as I passed it.

My aunt would tell me that Flight 93 had almost crashed while turning back east, quite low to the ground and almost at treetop level, three miles from the little town of Kipton, Ohio where I had spent my summers as a boy. This fact had not yet come out in the media, which had left the impression that the turn, before the passengers overtook the hijackers and crashed the plane in the Allegheny strip-mines of southern Pennsylvania, had occurred southeast of Cleveland.

Radio talk show host Rush Limbaugh would proclaim, "I don't care why these terrorists did it. They are nothing but thugs. I just want them brought to justice."

But for our own good, we need to understand why they did it. Insurance executives, particularly, have told the press that they thought that American politicians were as shocked as they were that attacks on this scale and with this kind of conspiratorial character (out of the spy novel genre) were even conceivable "in real life" in the American homeland. As my father told me when I was being thrown out of William and Mary in 1961 for telling the Dean of Men that I was gay, "We have to worry about what everybody thinks," even when we're morally right. Indeed we do.

The stock markets were closed for the rest of that terrible week and there were predictions of economic chaos. In the ensuing months the markets would recover (then flounder again in corporate scandals) even as layoffs rose sharply. The attacks may have shocked the markets into conceptualizing specific ways to recover, such as through infrastructure investment in security, air traffic control and defense, but some of this behavior is the normal way a business cycle works after a period of overcapacity. Though still employed as a salaried professional I got a taste of how the perception of my own marketability may have fallen when on Sept. 13 I received a call from a headhunter looking for commercial telemarketers!

POLITICAL CAUSES

We'll get into the psychology and religion shortly but it may be possible to explain much about the attacks in terms of more conventional politics. Actually, the world has seen guerilla, tribal, and terrorist warfare before—consider how World War I was launched.

The 9-11 attacks could be seen as an attempt by Osama bin Laden and his Nightbreed minions to force the United States to attack the Islamic world, and start a populist uprising among a huge population of poor, disadvantaged young Muslim men. The outrage would topple the royal family of Saudi Arabia so—guess who—gets to take over Saudi and the rest of the Islamic world. Perhaps Osama was throwing a temper tantrum because back in 1990 the Saudi family invited the United States to defend it from Iraq instead of its inviting bin Laden. By that view, this is mostly an intra-Islam conflict.

Ironically, falling oil prices in the late 80s could have made the Saudi royal family more vulnerable to fundamentalist and cleric Islamic dissidents. Even the Israel-Palestine conflict is a bit of a side show, as is bin Laden's claims about Americans killing Iraqi children. Actually Saddam Hussein is not particularly friendly to religious fundamentalism, and as of this writing the administration has denied direct evidence that he participated in the attacks, although he probably participated in money laundering operations, clandestine contacts, support for Palestinian suicide attacks and fomenting unrest among younger Saudi men.

We find that Saudi Arabia is not such a dependable friend.[21] The kingdom paid off blood money to religious clerics of Wahhabism and funded extremist schools in Afghanistan and Pakistan while the western world remains dependent on Saudi oil. Ultimately a shutoff of their oil, maybe much more prolonged than in 1973-1974, becomes a threat. We leave the rest of the world the impression that we will prop up any authoritarian regime that placates our gas-guzzling addiction.

The United States helped put the Taliban into power in Afghanistan after Osama bin Laden helped turn back Russia, which retreated from Afghanistan in 1989. The Clinton administration unwisely courted the Taliban because oil interests wanted to build an oil pipeline through Afghanistan. In its opposition to Communism, our own military advisors would locally ratify the more extremist Islamic idea that Allah pre-ordains one's assigned station in life, and most unfairly.

It is ironic that the Northern Alliance, seen now as an ally and liberating force, has had close ties to Communism. In fact, it too has been guilty of atrocities. In 1996 when the Taliban took over, the Taliban were seen as a law-and-order force, albeit one with extremist Islamic principles that would soon run amok. A permanent government in Afghanistan must represent all the ethnicities (and definitely include women). It is interesting to read the analysis of Afghan immigrant Tamim Ansary, "the email heard around the world," from Sept. 14, 2001.[22]

The recent tragedies in Israel and the West Bank (as of April 2002) show that some radicals will use any means—including relentless suicide attacks—to enforce a collective political goal. The peoples in the Middle East seem deeply rooted in collective tribal and religious identities, and yet the shame that they fight reaches deepest psychological levels.[23] CNN has reported about a Saudi Telethon where people from Saudi Arabia donate money, perhaps sacrificially, for Palestinians. At this point is was not clear whether any of this money was intended to compensate the families of martyrs. But the media has also reported that underground life insurance operations in the Middle East, particularly Iraq, have subsidized martyrdom.

On June 21, 2002, ABC's "20-20" with John Miller and Barbara Walters presented a bizarre story that suggested that members of Israeli intelligence photographed the striking and falling of the towers from the parking lot of a New Jersey high rise apartment building. This news story raises the troubling question that Israel might have experienced some bizarre political motive to draw the United States further into Mideast conflict. In late 2001, in fact, Barbara Walters had presented an interview with actor (producer and screenwriter) Matt Damon who related that the incident occurred on his first morning living in his new home in New York City. His story emphasized that absolutely anyone, no matter how famous or successful, could have become a victim of the tragedy.

Terrorism is sometimes described as the ultimate weapon of the weak, at least those without collectively provided advanced militaries. A terrorist fights with his untrimmed fingernails rather than his fists.

RELIGIOUS ARGUMENTS

Osama bin Laden's meandering religious arguments are really interesting. He considers Americans to be soiled, tainted softies, an easier enemy than the Russians. Along these lines, the Taliban has implemented views of gender roles and of the responsibilities of masculinity so draconian as to shock even most social conservatives—to the point of denying that any traditional idea of "family" can confer individuality regardless of station in life.

Perhaps our policy with Israel is motivated by the political influence of a powerful religious minority, and not by "lifestyle". Perhaps we say this even as we looked the other way while Israel violated the property rights (as a libertarian would understand them) of individual Palestinians going back to the time of Balfour. In 1948 Israel enacted legal expropriation of property and collectivization when less than 10% of the land was under Jewish control (Ahmad, discussed shortly[24]), and Israel increased this practice in the 1960s with the West Bank settlements. But why is it religious heresy for American troops (infidels, including, heaven forbid, female soldiers) to be stationed in the same country as Mecca? And, well, to bring up the Crusades—does something that happened 800 years ago have to be avenged now?

This gets closer to the argument, made by Andrew Sullivan, by *Rolling Stone*, and other progressive writers and publications that we ought to take the issues surrounding religious ideology much more seriously. Christianity at its best supports individualism, even among socially conservative branches (such as Mormonism, Southern Baptists, John Ashcroft's Assembly of God, and often enough Roman Catholicism). In these sects, individualism is mediated through the socializing influence of the traditional family and acceptance of divine prayer and direction. Judaism does this as well, but with much of Islam the importance of ritual (sometimes to the point of attending to matters like body hair) and a communal faith seems much more central to its teachings. Hence, consorting with unbelievers (infidels) or even allowing them to live in your part of the world could be seen as defiant to Allah.

Christianity and Judaism did inculcate the Greek Socratic tradition of individual truth-seeking that could augment a personalized faith. (The infidel argument from bin Laden reminds me of the military's idea that the mere presence of open gays in the ranks destroys unit cohesion.) Hence, the so-called *jihad* (if this term is acceptable) must become inevitable. (I speak in the subjunctive. The word "jihad" has been interpreted to mean a spiritual discipline, as with the well-known case of a Harvard University commencement speaker, as well as a militant misapplication of religious doctrine to gain or expand political control by force.[25])

The December 2001 *American Enterprise* contains contributions by Karina Rollins, Hillel Fradkin, and David Wurser that present the view of Islam as a publicly celebrated, imperialist religion, that will jump on apparent moral weaknesses of competing infidel societies that it believes it should subjugate, where political control through warrior-like behavior is part of the faith process. On the other hand, Niall Ferguson, writing in the *New York Time Magazine*, Dec. 2, 2001 places religious terrorism and war in the context of "fragmentation of multicultural polity." He conjoined this with globalization of terrorism, a second energy crisis, and "formalization of American imperialism." I tend towards more to this second view. It strikes me as curious that radical Muslim *mullahs* will state publicly and in a rather bald-faced manner that they aim to establish the superiority of their religion for its own sake. It is also interesting how radical Islam denies democracy as anti-Allah, whereas Judeo-Christian tradition promotes that democracy confers freedom for the individual to follow his own path of faith,

In fact, when addressing the Libertarian Party of Minnesota in April 2002, Dr. Imad-ad-Dean Ahmad characterized the history of Islam as one that started with a surprisingly libertarian view of the law, based on supply-side economics. Progressive Islamlic culture became corrupted over centuries by first social benevolence and then statism, and then presented a rather paradoxical view of church, state, and democracy in Islamic philosophy.[26] Islam had built a rather tolerant and progressive society, after all, in Spain during the first millennium.

On the other hand, there are numerous passages in the Koran, that taken out of context, would seem as vehement as the commandments in Leviticus in Judeo-Christian tradition.[27] A more balanced view of Islam may be available from books like *The Complete Idiot's Guide to Understanding Islam*,[28] which emphasizes the idea that hatred in the Islamic world is motivated in large part by Western aggression (such as taking land way from Palestinians) rather than religious ideology.

Indeed, libertarian commentators often emphasize that Islamic rage (their young men being "pissed") is the direct result of our interventions overseas in their largely religious affairs, rather than any aggressive intentions concern our own Western lifestyles. But for a significant portion of Islam, there seems to be an outlook that Islam must either conquer the known civilized world and convert it to Allah, or else sequester itself as if it were on another planet, safely light years away even from electronic influences.

There is an interesting observation that the Buddha statutes, archeological treasures a millennium before Mohammed, became "miners' canaries" when the Taliban destroyed them in 2000.

PSYCHOLOGICAL ARGUMENTS

Osama bin Laden's videotaped speech from the Jalalabad Caves on Oct. 7 (the day Bush ordered the bombing to commence) was broadcast worldwide. Its hatred, fervor and threats were chilling. It was if an alien intelligence had barged into our networks to sentence us to the Tribulations, even if his argument sound silly when looked at "rationally." Osama bin Laden has always struck me as a supernatural villain right out of Dean Koontz (not Tom Clancy or Clive Cussler).

And there is the suicide issue. We learn that in Palestine, Hamas approaches young men and bribes them to do suicide attacks by promising to pay off their families. Young men are supposed to be fungible, aren't they? (Read George Gilder.[29]) In this county, we have ourselves in the past conscripted those who would become cannon fodder.

So we learn that suicide in war against infidels is supposed to guarantee the young warrior an eternity in heaven. Okay, I can believe that this would appeal to the masses of disadvantaged young Muslim men, especially those educated in the *madrassahs*. But how do you explain Mohammed Atta, who lived the jet-set life for several years in Germany, Spain and the U.S. before flying a plane into the North Tower?

He grew up in relative privilege, almost to the point of spoilage. Psychiatrists say that he definitely knew what he was doing and understood right and wrong. Compared to domestic terrorists like Timothy McVeigh, Atta showed little psychiatric instability. Yes, there are reports of his religious *devotion*, especially when a graduate student in architecture in Germany. But in the end his behavior sounds like an exercise in nihilism, in sociopathy, of quitting when you're ahead, in suicide intended to make you famous and prevent your growing old in obscurity.

To me, he sounds not so different from Timothy McVeigh. It also seems to me that the kamikaze suicide attacks represent a culmination of increasingly bizarre cruelty and violence in a variety of hate-related crimes (the torture murder of Matthew Shepard, then Columbine) that occurred in the previous ten years in our own culture. Almost any act had again become thinkable.

The idea that the suicide hijackings could have been so cunningly pulled off by a platoon of nineteen men sounds shocking enough. Yet there are other reports of the behaviors of these men that sound shockingly arrogant, casual—the flight school (Atta almost got kicked out), the crop duster business attempts. ABC News reported that Atta apparently tried to get a loan for a crop duster business and that dispersal of chemical or biological weapons was probably his first choice. The interview with the government employee in Florida with whom Atta spoke was quite chilling. He first refused to speak to her because she was a woman. But he then spilled to her his cynical attitude towards American cities and landmarks.

Forensic psychologists described clinically the behavior of Osama bin Laden and his co-conspirators as that of people carrying out "overvalued ideas." Similar observations have been made about the Unabomber, Jack Kervorkian, and Timothy McVeigh #1. An associated concept is that of the *narcissistic personality*, an exaggerated and unjustified sense of self-importance bordering on sociopathy. The perpetrator know what he is doing and that it is wrong and criminal but believes the expression of his idea and his own recalculation of "morality" against that of society—particularly of the legal system—and even of the harm done to others ("collateral damage") justifies his behavior.

The perpetrator believes himself to be state-like. The imprint of the overvalued idea contributes to narcissism, so even a religious conviction—in a setting where religious faith is normally cherished—becomes overvalued if it leads to total disregard and insensitivity to others. The idea that one goes to heaven by killing other non-combatants for Allah is an example. Only law enforcement or military force can deter such individuals; normal ideas of therapy do not apply because the individual is not clinically ill in a normal clinical sense. Lesser variations of this behavior would involve doing something for a cause that the actor believes is likely to be viewed as wrong but during which the person does not directly harm others, steal, or commit actual violations of the law.

Moral teaching often involves *balancing* the hungers of the individual personality with meeting the real needs of others in manners not always chosen. Sexual morality seems to revolve around the idea that an individual gives up some independence (particularly as tied to experience through sexual excitement) in order to become tied to the requirements of family role and lineage or to meet one's religious calling. But religious fanaticism itself can become just as self-serving, a way to avoid family commitments to others or wield power over others. For insecure males fanatical religious ideology, which provides a motivational ideal as well as a group-identity point, can become as pleasurable as sexual pursuits. Marriage and family can easily become a hiding place from personal responsibility.

Were these attacks really an attack by one country against another, or more of one culture against individuals who practice another? It's both. Osama bin Laden had pretty much hijacked Afghanistan as a state for his own. His military force (based on Al Qaeda—also spelled Al Qaida— "The Base") is a loose confederation of semi-autonomous cells that combines individualistic autonomy with collective goals. His method of organizing seems bizarre in modern history but may have been practiced at various points in the past.

This hits at us in a more personal way, even if our concept of an enemy (like the word "Charlie" used to identify a guerilla enemy in Army Basic) is that of a collective entity. In his mind, the American government, the corporate state and citizens who enjoy its tainted fruits are one in the same. (We see that kind of thinking from the radical left.) But in the barest psychological terms, fundamentalist Islam seems to be defending a culture of exaggerated patriarchy where otherwise insecure men remain in control of their families and even harems.

Our idea of contagious freedom very much threatens that control. Even George Gilder would agree. Jonathan Rauch points out that leftist egalitarian nihilism and presumably rightist hierarchic religious extremism make temporary bedfellows in their common desire to attack the smugness of western individualism and even democratic capitalism[30].

Another way to look at this is to say that western openness and its tendency to broadcast its cultural pluralism will, in the minds of some people, threaten the very idea of using religious faith—especially when practiced as a public ritual—as the ultimate umpire of moral issues and as a brake against the individual competitiveness that implies that some people must accept "failure" on their own.[31] Western cultural openness, in this view, pokes fingers into the eyes of those of faith.

In the Spring of 2002, *The Weekly Standard* presented some more pointed interpretations. David Brooks would describe a social phenomenon of collective sweet lemons and sour grapes (I forget which term applies) as "bourgeoisophobia"—a self-righteous smug hatred of seemingly superficial, sometimes narcissistic commercial success comparable to the hatred of sissies or geeks by bullies,[32] and Dinesh D'Souza would characterize a religious tradeoff between virtue (and submission to Allah—religious authority) and freedom (with democracy, as well as acceptance of competition and failure) from the viewpoint of radical Islam.[33] Remember not all of Islam is ideologically so focused.

To me, the rage seen by some religious fundamentalists (and not just Muslims) seems to indicate a fear of psychological emasculation or loss of old-fashioned masculinity among men who depend upon control of their women and lineage for their sense of self worth. The "do ask, do tell" philosophy of gays' coming out (as in the military) and fighting for rights to be open corresponds to America's openness about its complicated culture (which is both materialistic and spiritual) and its tendency to boast (through movies, music and the Internet, even with sites like mine) in parts of the world unprepared to benefit easily from it.

On December 9, 2001, major news sources reported that a videotape exists in which Osama bin Laden is commenting on the September 11 attacks as they occur, and that bin Laden had not expected the Twin Towers of the World Trade Center to collapse to the ground, but only to the point of impact. On December 13, 2001 the tape was shown. It betrays a sadistic delight in the mayhem and in the fact that many of the Al Qaeda foot soldiers on the hijackings did not know that these were to be suicide missions.

It is not clear that the video was intended to be published and it would not be suitable for excerpted inclusion in a commercial documentary film (say, one built upon the experiences of various journalists). Again, it is very difficult for me to believe that this kind of psychopathology could be associated with any legitimate experience of religious faith, that it could be fundamental to Islam; it seems more to be fundamentally evil, as Laura Schlessinger of D. Scott Peck ("People of the Lie") would construe it.

Many commentators would offer particularly succinct statements as to what makes the terrorists tick, either from a "mean streak" (a phrase my own father liked to use) or essentially political motives. Salman Rushdie writes, "The fundamentalist believes that we believe in nothing. In his worldview, he has his absolute certainties, while we are sunk in sybaritic indulgences." Indeed, there are people, bound to creationism, who believe that teaching evolution undermines our ability to believe; some people perceive faith as necessarily and morally connected to narrow-mindedness and an unwillingness to receive more points of view.

Blaine and Robert Trump write, "Terrorist groups and rogue nations wish to defeat those different from themselves, those who hold different beliefs and are tolerant of others. Terrorists believe that the end justifies the means—any means." Indeed, terrorists deny any possibility of peaceful coexistence.

Bill Moyers writes, "But their real goal is to get inside our heads, our psyche, and to deprive us—the survivors—of peace of mind, of trust, of faith; they aim to prevent us from believing again in a world of mercy, justice, and love, or working to bring that better world to pass." Shashi Tharoor writes, "On September 11, 2001, the 21st Century was born...The terrorists failed to see their victims that way; they saw only objects, dispensable pawns in their drive for destruction."[34]

Yet Noam Chomsky, in a little booklet "9/11"[35] would offer a quite leftist interpretation half blaming global capitalism as well as previous American aggression, which he sees as having been reversed with shocking effect Mainland American had not been attacked by a foreign power since the War of 1812.

Our own president characterized the psychopathology by saying, "They hate those who are not like them." It's interesting to hear our own conservative right speak out against forced conformism.

ASSESSING THE THREATS

Please understand that what follows is a hypothetical, conjectural discussion. It is not a prediction. I do **not** at this time have secret or specific knowledge of threats. But I am worried. There is much that should be done to further defend again homeland threats (as was outlined in detail in a fall 2001 *Newsweek*). But it is also essential to eliminate all major operating cells overseas and evict from power all regimes that support them. There is really no choice about this. The administration is right about this.

Captured Al Qadea training manuals have underscored the determination of the enemy to enforce its views with asymmetric warfare and with an incredible amount of personal discipline required of members, including absolute secrecy and willingness to die as a religious martyr. One interesting point for an author and self-publisher like me is that the manuals are largely hand-written and were not efficiently printed, even though the organization obviously had the means to publish the manuals with economic efficiency. Lessons in the training camps often contained much oral memorization, and the lack of duplication was part of the secrecy plan.

On June 3, 2000, the Arab newspaper Al-Hayat quoted Sulaiman Abu Gaith as saying that more massive attacks on Americans and Jews were coming soon, and that they would exceed September 11. But the website (alneda.com) did not work. ABC News (using Associated Press reports) and "Good Morning America" made this a leading story that morning. Abu Gaith is a former Kuwaiti citizen who became associated with Al Qaeda.

Explosives

It is the evil determination of these terrorists and the vehemence of their compulsive destructiveness, when viewed psychologically, that forces us to assess the likelihood of future large-scale attacks and what would happen to our society if they were to occur.

To put things bluntly, the most grave threat is the nuclear one. This threat must be put into perspective. According to credible reports from Russian security advisors in the mid 1990s, over eighty Russian "suitcase nukes" (small nuclear weapons with heavy hydrogen detonation devices) are unaccounted for. Twenty-four more could be stolen from a volatile Pakistan. A suitcase nuke would vaporize an area the size of a baseball field and severely damage several square miles as well as permanently contaminate a much larger area downwind.

According to one report from the Center for Defense Information, over eighty of these weapons could be unaccounted for from stocks in Russia (they may be of varying size). Through the black market they could certainly fall into the wrong hands and someday be smuggled into the United States.[36] But it is likely that none of these devices could be detonated, as the tritium cores would have aged (although some military intelligence people tell me privately that terrorists could design crude replacements for these cores).[37]

A more likely plausible scenario would be the launching of "dirty bombs," conventional truck bombs laced with radioactive materials like uranium compounds, plutonium, or, perhaps more easily, materials related to medical use like cesium. On Dec. 3, 2001, the government admitted that Al Qaeda may be closer to developing dirty bombs than had been thought, and that they could have them in the United States, Saudi Arabia, or Europe.

Some of these, even with small detonations, could contaminate an area, enough to prevent rescue operations and cleanup. An area of some square miles (for example, around the White House or the Capitol) would be unusable commercially or residentially for decades or even centuries. Exposed people would be condemned to premature deaths from leukemias, lymphomas and lung cancers.[38] Dirty bombs are colloquially called "weapons of mass disruption," and many commentators claim that the actual health risks will be much less than what the media speculates. But the economic and ultimate long-term personal impact is so great that they should be regarded as weapons of mass destruction.[39] Terrorists could conceivably start a series of explosions, perhaps one per day or week, until political demands on the United States (like withdrawal from Saudi Arabia) were met. Supermarket tabloids (ironically the first targets of the anthrax attacks in October) love to warn that terrorists will attack and attack again whatever we do. (And, as films like *The Sum of All Fears* and *Bad Company* point out, other groups outside the Muslim world, such as neo-Nazis or various ethnic nationalists, might be capable of such nefarious intentions.)

However, it seems most unlikely given current evidence that many terrorists could have access to such weapons.[40] They would be extremely difficult for individuals or small cells to manipulate covertly without detection by law enforcement or without killing themselves. Most of the terrorists are of the "foot soldier" variety. Even so, to play devil's advocate, journalist Peter Bergen warned on MSNBC on November 30, 2001 that cells could be poised to deliver dirty weapons in a major event at the time that Osama bin Laden is captured or killed, a possibility that could lead the government to keep his death a secret and may help explain the government's aggressive use of "voluntary" roundup and interrogation.

A major piece in *Time* (3/11/2002)[41] relates an apparently unreliable report of a major Al Qaeda plot to smuggle a 10-kiloton nuclear device into New York City and suggests that future plots could be impossible to stop if terrorists are really determined. To their credit, the Customs Service and other law enforcement agencies are rapidly improving technology to detect routinely all kinds of dangerous cargo. The *Time* article also says that a coastal city could be destroyed by a liquefied natural gas explosion just off shore and questions whether current airline security technology could detect all hidden explosives.

On April 10, 2002, former Prime (Israel) Minister Benjamin Netanyahu warned the U.S. Senate that, just as the case with repeated Palestinian one-person suicide bombing attacks in Israel, suicide street-level bombings in public spaces, malls, theaters, or on subways, trains or busses could occur within the United States. He speculated that they could be coupled with weapons of mass destruction. Possibly random sniper attacks in the autumn of 2002 could be related to terrorist cells.

On April 22, 2002, a top Al Qaeda in military custody named Abu Zubaydah (the reporters did not say whether this was at Guantanomo, Cuba) taunted investigators with claims that the terrorist group is indeed very close to being able to build a dirty bomb and smuggle it into the United States. However, he may have been bragging to incite panic or to get more lenient treatment.[42] In June 2003 the government reported the military detention of American citizen Abdullah Al Muhajir (born Jose Padilla) who apparently was plotting to build a small dirty bomb and explode it in Washington, D.C. (this is discussed later). *Reader's Digest* published a fictitious but convincing scenario of how a dirty plutonium bomb could be planted in a large city by a terrorist (after smuggling materials from Russia) and how law enforcement would respond.[43]

Even purely conventional weapons could create havoc if used in subways or commuter trains. Even now security metal inspections are done for the Chunnel train between London and Paris/Brussels, and Americans face the difficult task of deciding whether we need to beef up detection on trains in our country. The worst thing about all of these explosives threats is that they can be launched covertly on the ground. They do not require planes or large platoon-sized teams.

A week before the Sept 11 attacks, *Popular Science* came out with an article claiming that inexpensive E-bombs (electromagnetic pulse) and *flux compression generator* bombs could be built by terrorists very cheaply. The claim was made that the whole country could be set back two hundred years by one blast. I sent an email about this to ABC Nightline, and a couple days later ABC posted a more temperate write-up on the issue. Ground "FCG" bombs (depicted at Las Vegas in the 2001 film *Oceans 11*) could not damage large areas, and data centers and communications centers could protect themselves with Faraday cages.

A more serious threat could be a high-altitude FCG explosion from a plane (or perhaps a small nuclear explosion). This observation means that it is imperative that airlines (or the federal government) begin screening all checked luggage as soon as possible (in advance of the November 19, 2002 deadline), even with decompression tests. Airlines will face other sudden challenges, such as the need to examine shoes (in light of an incident over the Atlantic in December) and the opportunity to use heat-sensing devices or pupilometrics as lie detection when asking security questions.

The difficulty of designing convincing defenses to all of these threats (along the lines or libertarianism) would, in my mind, I feel, justified the Bush administration's idea that overseas terrorist cells must be eliminated, along with the foreign regimes (like the Taliban and arguably Iraq) that support them. The administration's claim that terrorism is "non deterable" rings true. Of grave importance is tracking down nuclear (and, as below, biological and chemical) weapons anywhere in the world. And they will give considerable justification to domestic surveillance measures intended to detect and remove the cells.

We simply must not allow such attacks to happen. If they did, with major areas of the country uninhabitable or unusable, we really would loose our civil liberties as we know them (imagine the first day of national martial law). Libertarians have suggested that withdrawal from the Middle East should be done to remove the incentive terrorists have to make these threats.[44] But imagine an Osama bin Laden ruling Saudi Arabia (even assuming that we become independent of Arab oil) with access to nukes. Why would he not pursue his jihad, his compulsion now to convert the planet to Islam? Would such a regime be so irrational as to destroy the oil fields in some pretense of piety?

These possibilities are so horrifying that President George W. Bush now has enlarged his doctrine to stop not only those regimes that harbor terrorists or allow them to function but also those countries attempting to acquire weapons of mass destruction.[45] Along the lines of this argument, the debate over preemptively removing Saddam Hussein from power seems to be motivated more by the idea that Saddam, once he acquires nuclear weapons, will be able to attack and blackmail his neighbors than by any evidence of his direct involvement in 9-11, although it is likely that he was quite involved in money laundering and, as discussed below, some journalists believe that he could already be implicated in our anthrax attacks with his history of chemical attacks against his own people, the Kurds.

The attacks would, in at least one case to date, inspire tragic copycat behavior, when teenager Charles Bishop flew a light plane into a bank building in Tampa, Florida.

Bio-Terrorism

So far the country has experienced five deaths from anthrax. The pattern of anthrax by mail had not been predicted, but it might give clues to the terrorist motives.

In 1999, in fact, ABC's "Nightline" had rehearsed a scenario where terrorists release anthrax in a city subway system, and, given the unpreparedness of the public health system, 50000 deaths and total ruination of the city happen within a week. ABC would repeat an abbreviated version of this scenario on Friday, Oct. 5. I would get into a rather bizarre discussion of this right afterwards at a local gay bar in Minneapolis.

On Oct 10, authorities (led by U.N. inspector Richard Spertzel) reported that the Daschale letter contained professionally milled anthrax dust, more dangerous than the anthrax recovered from a letter received by Tom Brokaw a week before. It sounded like a terrorist playing games with us and planning the big one. So I angrily emailed ABC news and asked Koppel about the Oct. 5 broadcast. The next night Koppel interviewed HHS secretary Tommy Thompson and, referring to angry viewer concerns (like mine) over his earlier broadcast, reviewed the possibility of a mega-threat. Thompson tried to reassure the public that the public health service was now ready.

The evidence so far is that the incubation period for anthrax is much longer than had been expected, and that even inhalation anthrax (milder forms are gastrointestinal and cutaneous) is much more treatable than had been expected. Of course, we are not absolutely sure of the long-term prognosis for exposed people after they finish antibiotics. It also appears that elderly people are much more susceptible to smaller inhalations of spores. In time, the same observation may be found to apply to persons with reduced immune systems, such as those who are HIV-positive. This, along with mail cross-contamination, may explain some of the bizarre outlier cases encountered so far.

Authorities differ on whether finely milled anthrax potions could be made by domestic Unabomber-style terrorists. Preparation is supposed to be technically difficult and achievable only by governments. Because of reports of a meeting by Mohammed Atta with an Iraqi intelligence agent in 1999, there is considerable suspicion that the anthrax preparations could have been smuggled from Iraq. If so, this raises the grave possibility that Saddam Hussein is trying to wage covert asymmetric war with biological weapons. This would necessitate his removal from power after all.

Former congressman "B-1" Bob Dornan (no friend of my community) warned that Hussein would eventually try to mount huge casualties on the

United States if allowed to stay in power. There are detractors from this view, however, such as former U.N. weapons inspector Scott Ritter who made the film *In Shifting Sands* (2001). The very recent stories about Mohammed Atta's interest in obtaining funds for crop dusters reinforce the idea that anthrax or other biological or chemical weapons were available to him from overseas, especially Iraq.

But *The New York Times*, on Nov. 21, 2001, reported about a book by anti-government activist Timothy W. Tobiason on how to make anthrax and other biological and chemical weapons. Although its directions are reportedly inaccurate and crude, the book suggests that it may be conceivable that a homegrown terrorist (an individual sociopath like the Unabomber) could achieve such a production. The press has reported a USDA facility at the University of Iowa where a deadly preparation has existed since the 1950s (as it has at other universities) and this facility is easily viewed to the west of I-35, 30 miles north of Des Moines. Just before Christmas, the FBI reported that the anthrax could have come from a top-secret site in Nevada or in Ohio, and that a particular domestic scientist was under investigation.[46]

If a terrorist had expected to cause mass casualties with anthrax, it seems that he has run out of time. Even a subway attack would likely be observed by police, resulting in shutdown (maybe an immediate arrest) and there would be much more time for preventative treatment than had been expected. Still, it would be prudent for American metro systems to start putting in hardened plastic suicide panels like those in London and Paris to prevent materials from being thrown onto tracks in front of trains.

While addressing a convention of the Libertarian Party of Minnesota in April 2002, state representative Richard Mulder, M.D. (Republican, also a family physician) suggested that a substantial number of domestic research professionals probably have access to anthrax and the technical capability to mill it into a lethal weaponized form. This claim contradicts major media reports, and wind would quickly disperse almost any conceivable outdoor release of an agent.

Another medical professional here told me, however, that manufacture was extremely difficult indeed and that most likely the perpetrators had simply run out of their supply and could not replace it. In April 2002 David Tell provided a detailed examination of the anthrax investigation to date, and again keeps alive the strong possibility that the anthrax really did come from Iraq or Russia.[47]

I had a conversation in, of all places, the Saloon (a Minneapolis gay night club) with Minneapolis mayor Sharon Sayles Belton. She indicated that the biggest fears from public health officials now were smallpox and plague. One could add botulism toxin to this list, since this substance is by weight one of the deadliest known. But in two months the public health system has made considerable progress in rapidly building up vaccine re-stocks to use in the event of even one smallpox case. Even now, unless there were a large number of index cases in a short time, it should be possible to isolate the victims and vaccinate large numbers of contacts.

Laurie Garrett provided a sobering discussion of bio-terrorism in the December 2001 issue of *Vanity Fair*. Other possible agents include botulism, and the Marburg and Ebola viruses. In 1978 Stephen King wrote a novel, *The Stand*, where a government experiment accidentally creates a "superflu" virus that kills 99% of the world's population. As of this writing, there is no clear-cut way a sexually transmitted disease like HIV could be weaponized to produce rapid casualties, although in the 1980s some people actually suspected that HIV resulted from bio-engineering aimed at gay men and other groups.

There have been close to a hundred arrests for anthrax "hoaxes," including those where persons have placed harmless powders in mail pieces, or even posted jokes on their own properties in connection with Halloween. The simple act of assembling a mail piece could conceivably pose a risk for accidentally creating the appearance of a hoax. This seems almost Kafla-esque, but in time of war extreme penalties are sometimes necessary, just as laws regarding jokes at airports must be enforced rigorously.

I do **not** have any specific knowledge of secret or unapproved treatments for biological, chemical or nuclear agents.

TARGETING

As already noted, many observers feel that the Al Qaeda attacks were directed more at the United States government or large visible corporations as retaliation for American foreign policy. Others feel that the attacks are directed against American lifestyle values that encourage a tainted self-expression and differentiation outside of religion (and these values are connected to democracy, which radical Islam may view as idolatrous).

At the same time an authoritarian, static religious hierarchy would prevent infidels from hiding behind secular institutions (even marriage) and having things that they do not deserve. Recent FBI reports suggest that terrorists could target ordinary Americans in lifestyle-related places: public spaces, theaters, subways, hotels, apartment residences, and shopping malls. One advantage for terrorists might be the relative lack of security in most such spaces and the possibility that a low-tech attack could cause enormous disruptions.

Already theaters in some metropolitan areas have banned backpacks and containers, and some public concerts (like 'Nsync) were conducting entry security before 9-11. Apartment property managers now generally check passports and visas or ID's from rental applicants carefully, and Hotels generally require passports from foreign tourists. If terrorists were able to undermine the confidence that ordinary Americans (and Europeans, Canadians, etc.) can carry out their own lives (and retain their own "secular" personal motivations), the economy and government would, in their view, become undermined. But this is already being tried in Israel big time.

In mid May, 2002, major press sources (including *Time* and *Newsweek*) ran detailed stories as to whether the Bush administration had not come clean about what it may have known before 9-11-2001, or whether it had failed to connect the dots. The CIA and FBI had a variety of leads, some of which pointed to more conventional terrorism (taking hostages for political negotiation) and others which frankly suggested suicide attacks and ramming planes into buildings. If you combine their intelligence with what various journalists had known since the late 1990s, there is little question that we should have foreseen this kind of attack. The government does not seem sanguine that future attacks can be prevented.

Particularly galling, apparently, is the way the FBI shelved (and perhaps manipulated) the memo from Minneapolis FBI agent Coleen Rowley in August 2001 regarding the handling of Zacarias Moussaoui.[48] Then *Newsweek* would report on the failure of the CIA to properly pass on information about future hijackers attending a terrorits' meeting in Malaysia in early 2001.[49] On May 29, 2002 the FBI announced a large reorganization and administrative rules changes that would allow FBI agents to attend and monitor public spaces and public Internet sites (including mine). Of course, a writer who self-publishes should welcome anyone (including law enforcement) to read his publicly available work In early June President Bush asked Congress to help him create a cabinet department for Homeland Security (parallel to Treasury, Justice and Defense).

The ensuring debate emphasized that the FBI may have had the raw data that it needed, but it lacked the analytical and information technology methods to relate tips.

CIVIL LIBERTIES, GOVERNMENT, AND NATIONAL SECURITY

There is no question that government is going to be much more involved in homeland national security than we had ever expected, and libertarians will not be comfortable with this. Already, federal laws have been passed that require most airport security scanners to become federal employees (without the usual civil service protections). Billions will be spent on various national defense and cyber security projects, and in sanitizing and protecting the mail. Government will become much more visible as an employer (both of military, civilian civil service and contractors), and background investigations and security clearances will become much more important as employment issues.

Training and compensating passenger security screening people as professionals is certainly a welcome and necessary step (to be paid for by passengers), but this measure raises a subtle issue about background checks. The requirements that screeners (and other airport employees with access to secure areas) be citizens and perhaps pass rather invasive questioning may become controversial.

There will be passenger concerns about invasion of privacy, particularly with pat-down body searches (where there are now, in early 2002, scattered complaints of abuses) as well as see-through technology. The government will allow passengers to be screened by employees with the same gender, but what about passengers (hopefully few) who might expect reassurance that a screener is not gay? This raises questions reminiscent of the military gay ban in suddenly important civilian security jobs (although these concerns have been visited before in areas like medicine and patient examinations).

Government is also involved in bailouts of industries disproportionately affected by terrorism, especially airlines and insurance industries. These settlements may have been designed to limit the airlines' exposure to litigation, especially in that one can claim that the government was really the terrorists' intended target and that government shared heavily in the failure to prevent the attacks with proper coordination of intelligence. Businesses have taken the (questionable) position that the attacks were primarily aimed at government and that therefore government should indemnify businesses and citizens against the tremendous losses.

Libertarians have debated whether the tort system would be adequate to handle the liability issues that stem from the attacks. Insurance coverage for the enormous damage from terrorists probably will not be available without government backing. The attacks seem counter to the idea of urban culture and high-density living and working, so important to an open, pluralistic culture. Negligence tort law will have to evolve in areas like determining what kinds of risks businesses and governments can anticipate.

Immigration is an obvious target among libertarian positions. Government will enforce immigration law much more vigorously, and persons of Middle-Eastern origin will be unfairly singled out.

But the biggest problems regard government actions that jeopardize the privacy, due process, and free speech of ordinary citizens. The proper balance in these matters, especially in regard to the Constitution and Bill of Rights, must be examined closely. Furthermore, the sensible expectations of both businesses and of individuals in this changed world of asymmetric war must be elucidated.

In October 2001 Congress passed the USA Patriot Act with little debate. The act's full name is The Uniting and Strengthening of America by Providing Appropriate Tools Required to Intercept and Obstruct Terrorism Act of 2001. In this act, law enforcement was given new powers and means for surveillance (with techniques like pen registers) of telephone calls, emails, and web surfing with greatly reduced judicial supervision. There is at least a slight risk (the "Daniel Ellsburg problem") that even the physical residences and offices (including computer hard drives) of ordinary citizens could be searched (and damaged) with less court supervision then in the past, when terrorism—with a rather expansive definition to include most asymmetric violent threats and even computer crime—is suspected.

Electronic Frontier Foundation has produced a thorough and critical analysis of this law at its web site;[50] there are genuine constitutional questions about possible abrogations of the 4th and 5th Amendments in the legislation. More important may be the practical questions. Most ordinary Americans, even those like me who are politically or vocally active in a civil and responsible manner probably won't be compromised right now. But the slope is indeed slippery.

In the beginning, those targeted are likely to be mostly those of Middle Eastern origin, mostly non-citizens, and they will sometimes be arrested for trivial law violations. Down the road you have a scenario where persons suspected of unproven terrorist associations are picked up and held for, say, marijuana possession.

It is a well-known law enforcement principle, effectively practiced in New York by Giuliani) that you prevent big crimes (violence and burglary) by cracking down on the little ones, (graffiti, vandalism, speeding, minor drug offenses, soliciting prostitution). Police statistics in many cities support this idea. But applied to terrorism the dangerous implications are clear. What if down the road gays become politically vulnerable, and spreading a fatal sexually transmitted disease is equated to terrorism?

There has even been a controversy over seeking checkout records from public libraries of weapons-related books, at least in Florida. State laws generally protect the confidentiality of records of what public library patrons check out. It does seem that most public libraries would not carry books that they knew gave very explicit directions on how to deploy or build weapons of mass destruction. Most responsible publishers or web operators will not supply such information (I do not). The American Booksellers Foundation for Free Expression (ABFFE) and more recently the American Library Association report that the government can even demand that libraries and booksellers provide the names of persons who have borrowed purchased books on certain kinds of weapons.[51]

The government maintains that, under the Patriot Act, it will only seek such records (or comparable internet records from ISP) concerning individuals for whom there is a limited probable cause of suspicion for involvement in terrorist conspiracy. Libraries, booksellers and ISP's are required to keep customer lists secret. Some of this disclosure attempt reminds one of the "know your customer" requirements in banking, but in the intellectual property world such requirements would have a chilling effect on speech.

Surveillance issues continue to mount. There are scattered reports of individuals being investigated by the FBI or Secret Service for possessing literature or posters extremely disparaging to the president.[52] In July 2002 the government announced that it wanted to expand its volunteer TIPS program to enlist various workers (even postal workers) who often enter homes and businesses or deliver items as possible informants, and this obviously raises genuine Fourth Amendment and probably cause issues; many individuals receive items like ads for weapons because of indirect marketing association.

It may be acceptable (although maybe only after a constitutional amendment) to reduce the standard for probable cause specifically for terrorist offenses alone. Terrorism would be defined as the intentional infliction of injury or loss of life upon non-combatants within the United States or allied countries as a political or social protest. By this principle, information gathered by pen-registers or by Carnivore (without normal juridical oversight) could not be used for drug prosecutions or even for something like child pornography—only for terrorism.

Conservatives maintain that terrorist motives increase the justification for the death penalty (and sometimes military tribunals) in violent crimes. If so, hate crime sentencing could logically be looked at for increased penalties, even though conservatives and libertarians have resisted hate crimes laws on the theory that they make a criminal sentence dependent upon the victim rather than the act itself.

Despite the claims of the 2002 movie *Collateral Damage*, there at first seemed to be little connection between the drug cartels and terrorists. Some news accounts credit the Taliban with cracking down on opium growing while they were in power, but others have accused them of taking advantage of the trade. However in time connections are likely to be shown. In November 2002 the attorney general announced several indictments regarding drugs for big-time weapons deals, and CNN may have just uncovered a connection between drug cartels and 9-11. But then you have a situation where drug laws, by creating an enormous profit incentive, set up a situation where terrorists could build alliances and cover. Drug laws could actually be seen as counter to the best interests of national security. Drug enforcement resources could be spent specifically on detecting weapons of mass destruction.

And let us again consider weapons and screening. Many of the new airport security measures will make little difference. The simple fact is that had pilots been allowed to arm themselves (even just with stun guns) and had cockpits been protected by locked reinforced doors before September 11, these kinds of attacks simply could not have happened, although in time other kinds of attacks probably would have. (Some accounts report that pilots were drawn out of the cockpits to come to the aid of flight attendants.) Even among passengers the capacity for self-defense has gained new public respect. Todd Beamer and gay rugby player and body builder Mark Bingham, by attacking the hijackers, helped prevent the last plane from making it to Washington and crashing into the Capitol. Otherwise the Air Force would have had to shoot the plane down, leading to another horrible spectacle. *Barron's* has called for the posting of two armed air marshals on every domestic flight (not just those using Reagan National in Washington) as an economic necessity.[53] In July 2002 Congress was still debating arming pilots. Not even Israel does this.

European airport security has long been much tighter than American security, to the point that I had to be body-searched in Amsterdam because of a metal plate in my hip. Yet there is little sense of intrusion or inconvenience at the major European airports where better security has become efficient. No, we probably don't need the profiling and intensive interviews of Israeli airport security. But one wonders how we got to the point that box cutters and knives could be carried on board airplanes when discos and rock concerts screen attendees for all weapons.

Would a national-ID system or international system with a biometric base make travel and entry to sensitive areas safer? It might reduce identity theft but it might also lead us to confuse identification with trustworthiness.[54]

In November, President Bush would add controversy by ordering that the United States have the capacity to try foreign terrorists with military tribunals. These military judicial procedures offer reduced due process, less protection of *habeas corpus*, information for defendants, attorney-client privilege, unanimous verdicts, standard of proof beyond a reasonable doubt, lack of right of appeal, dependence upon the Uniform Code of Military Justice (UCMJ), and the like (and the protections of the accused may even be less than usual in the U.S. military, such as the right to know full details of the charges).

Originally, this measure could not apply to non-citizens. I think that it should not apply to citizens fighting in foreign armies whether as mercenaries or because of personal ideology. Citizens should always have the full protection of the procedures of the normal criminal justice system. However, as noted above, on June 10, 2002 the government announced that it was holding a US citizen Abdullah Al Muhajir (born Jose Padilla) in military custody as an unlawful combatant. Investigation showed that he had allegedly been communicating with Al Qaeda in Pakistan. This "coronary bypass" of normal civilian procedural due process is argued to be constitutional according to the powers given Congress (Article I, Section 8) and the Executive to conduct war, maintain the armed forces and militia. (It appears that U.S. citizens who are deemed as unlawful combatants might be held during an armed conflict without charge, although it appears questionable that they can actually be tried under the UCMJ by military tribunals unless they are actually in the uniformed armed forces of another country or have formally lost citizenship.) Some scholars point out that only Congress has this power, however, and that the President has overstepped his bounds in issuing this order on his own.

Of course, one has to accept the idea that the war against terrorism, conducted on the home front, is still war in the domestic legal sense. It is difficult to argue with the need to keep judicial proceedings related to supposed terrorist plots secret as part of further intelligence operations, or even to protect juries or trials from becoming terrorist targets. Again, you have to define foreign terrorism as war and foreign terrorists as combatants.

Even more disturbing is the detention of up to 5000 foreign nationals without charge. (Is this, "do what you have to do but don't tell me?") Remember the mistakes of the past, too, the internment of the Japanese Nisei during World War II.

Civil libertarians like Julian Epstein have already pointed out that existing laws such as FISA (Foreign Intelligence Surveillance Act) provide a mechanism to conduct constitutionally fair trials with proper protections for the accused as well as protection of intelligence. Epstein also points out (on CNN) that although Bush's order originally (until Padilla) applied only to non-citizens, the Supreme Court has previously said that this kind of order is possible even for citizens who behave as foreign combatants (despite constitutional procedural due process [Amendments 5, 6, and 14] provisions), and a future president could possibly enact such a measure against citizens as a "drug exception to the Bill of Rights." What then about public health?

In December 2001 the Bush administration narrowed the order to guarantee that unanimous verdicts are still required for the death penalty and that most other procedural safeguards, other than rules regarding hearsay evidence, would be followed in the tribunals. But it also has since held at least one citizen (Padilla, noted before) as an unlawful combatant without charge.

The *New York Times* has presented analysis that divides the most serious constitutional problems into three areas: (1) Secrecy in the courts, especially with respect to immigration violations; (2) the detention of material witnesses for a long time before any criminal charges; (3) the indefinite length of some detentions (of at least two United States citizens) as unlawful combatants, with compromised legal representation, with a ruling by the Fourth Circuit affirming the commander in chief's right to detain combatants who take up arms against the United States.[55]

The trial—which will be a conventional civilian trial with due respect for classified information procedures—of Zacarias Moussaoui may provide an object lesson in the standard of evidence needed to hold someone. Moussaoui, recall, was arrested in August 2001 in Minnesota on immigration violations after suspicious behavior at a flight school. As noted in the Rowley memo, the FBI, three weeks before the attacks, did not find legal probable cause to look at his computer hard drive.

Hindsight here must be painful. No amateur would have interest just in steering a jetliner unless he had intended to bring one down upon a target; that's common sense. The government already knew a lot about Osama bin Laden from his attacks in Africa and Yemen, and the World Trade Center had been attacked in a clumsy way in February 1993 (ironically about the same time that the military gay ban debate erupted in the new Clinton administration) by someone with distant ties to bin Laden.

Furthermore, a number of journalists such as Sebastian Junger (US) and Peter Berger (Britain) had traveled to Afghanistan and other trouble spots to study terrorists and especially Osama bin Laden, other Al Qaeda leaders and the Taliban, including the war against it by the Northern Alliance. (Junger and Bergen have both written about the strategic importance of Massoud, assassinated Sept. 9, 2001, in helping bring down the Soviet Union.) The work of these journalists suggests a developing privately held but well published concern that "organized terrorism" would take truly sinister turns. Ted Koppel had long aired broadcasts on bioterrorism. It was not asking too much for the government to consider all of this together and realize that the Moussaoui arrest in August amounted to a national emergency. How many of us private citizens with moderate levels of political involvement might have gotten bizarre emails, which we deleted as junk without reading them, that might have been disguised attempts by plotters to find out if their plans were leaking? I recall two such emails.

The charges against American John Walker Lindh have produced controversy. Many Americans resent the way that he seemed to thumb his nose at the freedom with which he was apparently raised. In one brief interview, Walker indicated he had been speaking mostly Arabic for months before his discovery and that most Muslims seek martyrdom (not objectively true). Some people wanted to charge him with treason, but this criminal conviction (usually reserved for defected agents like Aldrich Ames in 1994) requires, according to the Constitution, direct testimony by two witnesses of overt acts or confession in open court.

Attorney General Ashcroft filed serious charges calling for life without parole, and Ashcroft talks as if Walker made deliberate choices to fight with an enemy of America. However, it sounds unlikely that Walker could have grasped the consequences of what he was doing when he moved about in Yemen and Pakistan to follow what he saw as a demanding spiritual practice. His case will raise serious conceptual questions ranging from freedom to worship to the meaning of loyalty. (In July 2002 Lindh pleaded guilty to two counts for a twenty year sentence, and as part of the agreement he was told he could be held as an unlawful combatant if he ever engages in terrorist associations after his release.)

Much closer to home are concerns over freedom of speech. No, not just surveillance of personal emails, but also the possibility that cottage self-publishing on the Internet and in books could be perceived as a security threat Perhaps this is an exaggerated concern. After all, a message board, book, or website is out in the open, so how can it be a threat to security?

There are several concerns. The largest concern is steganography, the practice of sending coded messages with simple images or slogans (as was common with runners in ancient times) or of hiding complex instructions in encrypted links hidden behind innocuous images. The sheer volume of individually owned websites, chat rooms and message boards makes it possible for a terrorist to set up a domain for steganographic communications. A terrorist might hack into a web site owned by an unsuspecting person or small business without elaborate firewalls, security and geeky technical monitoring skills. A terrorist could spoof (or "heckle") another person as the sender of email when making threats, and then there would occur the question as to whether the audit trails of such email messages would always clear the target of blame.

Another large concern is the publication of instructions on killing or how to make weapons of mass destruction. I have been involved in litigation involving Internet censorship related to sexually explicit content, but from a national security perspective, we have realized (ever since Jonesboro and Columbine) that some unsavory individuals may use the Internet to plan violent behavior, particularly hate crimes. There has been legal controversy over whether ISPs could be held liable for what their customers publish (are ISPs "utilities" or "publishers"?) and the recent growth of on-demand cooperative publishing raises questions about the ability of fast-track publishers to take responsibility for negligent publication by their authors.

Columnist Walt Brasch points out that the proposed capability for government to obtain library checkout records or Internet surfing records may make publishers (both print and web) less inclined to handle controversial material (and perhaps liability insurance companies less willing to insure authors and publishers who provide it).[56] These concerns all have the capability to shut down a lot of pseudo-commercial speech—very valuable but not as professionally managed or profitable—growing today.

Earlier wars were marked by sedition acts, as during World War I when journalists could be jailed by sedition laws for criticizing the draft. In earlier times, free speech was considered dangerous because the public was considered easier to manipulate and because critical speech was considered to give aid and comfort to the enemy. Even now, some liberal commentators claim that the establishment press is muzzled by the Bush administration.

In the age of the Internet, the public is given more credit by politicians for being able to think for itself. That is seen as good to a point, especially in a terrorism crisis where alertness of individual citizens is an important part of national security. Almost anyone leading an active social or professional life could accidentally stumble upon evidence of terrorism or become a target. The gay community could be exposed because it is so socially fluid. The idea that a "closeted" domestic terrorist-cell member could want to "defect; sounds plausible to me.

Does talking freely and publicly about possible threats give terrorist ideas or play into their games? Time, discussion and information are on the side of the good guys (and gals). I can only quote Laurie Garret writing in detail about bioterrorist threats: "The very writing of this article is, then, an arduous exercise in the ethics of truth, restraint, balance, and justifiable alarm." (*Vanity Fair*, Dec. 2001, p. 198). Echo. But there is a possibility that statements made by less-established self-instantiated individuals (compared to well-known news and lobbying organizations) may have more targeted effects on some terrorist-leaning readers.

In fact, I have thought that the pervasivity of American and western speech, in broadcast media and by average citizens on the Internet, would reach that part of the world as an influence for political moderation and democracy. And we have found such poverty and deliberate intimidation by authoritarian regimes that this has not happened much—many citizens in these countries do not have computer access.

The "aid and comfort" problem has also surfaced in another way, as private organizations have created Internet sites blacklisting individuals (especially academia) who colorfully criticize America's efforts to fight back. On a few campuses and other employers, professors or employees have been disciplined for aggressive speech (both overly patriotic and disloyal speech). Legal writers have warned employers not to go overboard on suppressing the expression of opinions on this by staff, even to some extent at work. At a commencement speech in Sacramento, CA a newspaper president was booed off the podium for suggesting (in the view of patriotic students) that threats to civil liberties need to be discussed systematically.

"Expressive association" (the concept ironically so fundamental to the Supreme Court's ruling in *Dale v. Boy Scouts of America* and in GLIL's [Gays and Lesbians for Individual Liberty] brief actually arguing the BSA position) comes under question in anti-terrorism. Non-citizens, at least, may he held for associating with foreign groups advocating terrorist agendas without having made specific threats. This may be a legal extension of the concept that it is a crime to plot to overthrow the government of the United States or of any state. According to one report, a passenger was denied boarding on a flight because of her position in the Green Party, and of the Green Party's reported position against American retaliation overseas against the Taliban.

Another adjunct of the association problem will be profiling, as with the unfortunate incidents where young men with Middle Eastern names or physical appearances are detained at airports. As a gay man, I know profiling from another angle: in the late 1980s, I found that being a never-married man pegged me as a health insurance risk when job-hunting, and I suppose you can construct an associational behavioral rationalization for this as just. As noted above, investigating associational behavior raises 4th Amendment and due process problems.

Citizens would understand that they have a legal responsibility to dissociate themselves from terrorist associations that they may accidentally encounter. This happened to me once in December of 1972 (three months after the Munich Olympics attacks). I had been associating with the Peoples' Party of New Jersey, when suddenly it advocated the use of violent protests. I quickly drop all contact with them, but soon "came out"—a critical time of my own life. Of course, that organization was hardly capable of carrying out anything more than their silly lettuce boycotts. People today will have to be more careful about future downstream liability for their associations and for the consequences of careless remarks overheard or misunderstood by others.

The Patriot Act does contain one provision that may undergo First Amendment scrutiny. It is an offense (for an author, publisher, webmaster, etc.) to publish an assembly of directions for making a weapon of mass destruction, even if the components of the published material came from freely available, unclassified sources, when the publisher has reason to believe that a terrorist will (using this information in combination, following a well known idea in security classification circles) be able to make such a mass destruction weapon and is likely to use it, even if such use is not "imminent" (following the "imminent threat of lawless action" in incitement cases, a doctrine easily used to regulate speech at airports, for instance).

The problem here is the converse of "legitimate value when taken as a whole" doctrine used in obscenity and sometimes in harmful-to-minors cases. Here, the component pieces may be lawfully published separately if an individual is unlikely to find them all, whereas they may not be lawfully published together in one work (or as one website), an observation with clear First Amendment problems. This does bring to mind civil litigation in cases where books have allegedly promoted crimes, such as with the Paladin case.

The Patriot also contains a provision that a business owner who allows (through failing to practice proper security) a server or web domain to be hijacked for secondary cyber terrorist attacks on critical government or commercial infrastructure may face criminal (or, presumably, civil charges) leading to imprisonment, fines of $10,000 and court injunctions shutting down his business. (Some legal experts, as at Electronic Frontier Foundation, have told me that these fears may be exaggerated.) Commercial anti-virus software may not always catch zombie Trojans planted by hackers even when the software is properly updated, and small business owners could be pressured to hire special security consultants as part of their due diligence.[57]

Presumably, as already noted, for web domains hosted by commercial ISP's the legal downstream liability lies with the host ISP, but then an ISP could fear a customer whose controversial editorial content might attract attacks. The FBI has discovered evidence of Al Qaeda reconnaissance of critical infrastructures in the United States (dams, nuclear power plants) through the Internet, both for downloading basic security information and to discover infiltration points.[58] Yet one wonders why, say, the operations of a nuclear power plant would have an IP node accessible (potentially to hackers) to the public Internet.

Free speech has an important upside for security—that the public ought to be much better informed about any trouble spot in the world. Serious national security threats could come from Russia (if it were to revert), Bosnia, China (with respect to Taiwan and even Tibet), India v. Pakistan, a coup in Saudi Arabia, the Palestinian problem, North Korea, even Sierra Leone. Foreign affairs tend to present problems in terms of nationalities and groups, and yet this crisis has turned into one of a mistrust of individualism. For both communism and religious hierarchialism share the desire to hide the individual from his own competitive failures.

And, not least, there is growing discussion of the possibility of conscription, to renew the draft (not used since Nixon stopped it in 1973). Congress still has the right to do that, and the Selective Service System is still in place to build contingent lists for induction, and draft age men are still required to register. Michigan Senator and Armed Services Chairman Carl Levin suggested that on CNN on Sept. 14, and Charles Moskos argued in *The Washington Post* (Nov. 4) that some sort of national service conscription (with non-military options available) will be needed for homeland defense. Even Bob Dole recognized the possibility on Larry King Live on Nov. 20.

In *Do Ask, Do Tell* I had included making conscription, which I compared to involuntary servitude, unconstitutional as the aim of an amendment. Now I believe that it may be constitutionally acceptable when the homeland is directly attacked or is genuinely threatened with weapons of mass destruction from a foreign (or even extraterrestrial) source, which it is now. Presumably, such a draft would also involve women (though that would require a new law). If constitutional and legal, is the draft really a good idea now?

Now, there are real questions about how many homeland security duties could be done by non-professional conscripts (certainly not special operations overseas). The Pentagon is against the idea, although one could construe the contingent possibility of a military draft—with male-only specific combat assignments and deployments allowed when necessary— as a possible component of deterrence against some kinds of enemies, including those who would wage asymmetric warfare. The Clinton administration had declined the idea of doing away with Selective Service altogether because of concerns over staff in medical and computer warfare staffing.

Another issue (curiously not mentioned by Moskos) is how the military gay ban and "don't ask, don't tell" would play out. As a matter of law, a recruit whose unrebutted statements indicate a propensity to engage in homosexual acts must be denied entry into the military (non-military services might be a different matter). Younger gay men have been asking me this repeatedly. As I argued in my books, the ban is itself (whether "don't ask don't tell" or whether there is required self-outing and asking) a potential security threat, and it would further compromise the lives of gay people (especially men) outside of the military. I emailed Moskos on this, and he wrote back, "**Gays must come out for conscription. Then the ban would be lifted**." In any case, a return to the draft of compulsory national service (Moskos suggests eighteen months) would slow the tide of tremendous teen successes in recent years: the music business (yup, I admired Naptser), boy bands, even high tech security companies. Imagine young men who have already decorated themselves with body art and tattoos being drafted.

In December 2001, Moskos would add a counterpoint (balanced by an opposing view from Lawrence Korb) that resuming the draft was an almost mandatory necessity, that conscripts could be used for the labor-intensive portions of civilian airport security, and that (this disturbs me particularly because of the downstream social implications) the military draft would remain male-only.[59] The draft would change some of the psychological balance in the rift between generations, and make age a better thing again.

Here, it strikes me that the mood of victory in the period after the 1991 Persian Gulf War and the impression that we easily enjoyed national security made a debate over gays in the military more credible in mainstream American culture. Ten years before (as AIDS seemed out of control and as the religious right was gaining influence in the Reagan years) it would not have been thinkable. It should be noted that civilian forms of draft exist. In Israel, parents must spend a certain amount of time provide security at schools. Even Moskos has suggested non-military alternatives to satisfy a draft requirement, maybe with fewer benefits, but of particular interest to many women and perhaps to non-combative men.

If we really do have major attacks in the future or lose control of our homeland security, we could wind up like the freedom fighters in the 1984 film *Red Dawn*: we give up our plans, purposes and agendas for ourselves, and hope that our children, collectively, have better lives in the next generation—if we win eventually. Isn't that how war can go? But then the question arises—may government curtail civil liberties temporarily with a sunset provision, or until a crisis is over? May the "fundamental" character of some rights be dependent upon a time axis with a national security crisis? Charles Krauthammer has bluntly written that a handful of terrorists with suitcase nukes or dirty bombs could destroy America.[60] This crisis will go on for a long time.

In fact, the Bush administration admitted in March 2002 that it has resurrected a "shadow government" of government officials who live in shelter facilities, away from their families for ninety days at a time. This is an expansion of the FEMA civilian reservist programs set up in the 70s and 80s for the Cold War.[61] It was not announced where these facilities are, but they could include Mount Weather in the Virginia Blue Ridge between Va-7 and US-50 (busy when I drive past it), or even the Greenbrier in White Sulphur Springs, W. Va, which I visited and toured in 1997. Is this a military-style life for civilians, living essentially in barracks and not going home at night? Does this invoke "don't ask, don't tell"?

I'll add here that the gay community is no stranger to terrorism. In 1973, over twenty men were burned to death when a gay bar in New Orleans was fire-bombed. There was a bombing of a gay bar in Atlanta in 1996 after the Olympic Park bombing, and a plot to blow up a gay disco in Seattle in 1998. The 1998 torture-murder of Matthew Shepard in Wyoming, even if directed at one individual, was a grim warning of where hatred could lead. One could make similar observations about murders of African-Americans and of attacks against abortion clinics. So far these have all been domestic.

An important issue to gays and lesbians is payment of benefits to domestic partners of heroes in the Sept. 11 catastrophe. In May 2002 the House of Representatives pulled a bill (at the instigating of "Barney Fag" Dick Armery) that would have extended benefits to non-spousal or legally or blood related persons if those persons were named in the wills of the deceased. Later, however, the Mycal Judge Act was passed to allow such benefits.

WHAT SHOULD BUSINESSES AND INDIVIDUALS EXPECT?

The government is saying, live normally, even has a very stirring music video produced with a travel council. Sometimes it seems to be claiming that consumerism and shopping normally is a patriotic duty. I even had such a conversation with Minnesota Governor Jesse Ventura at the Sept. 22 Human Rights Campaign dinner (about airlines and fear of flying). Having traveled some in Europe recently, to places like Auschwitz and to Bilbao, Spain (for the Guggenheim), located in areas with severe past problems, I can say that security over there is much tighter, but it is not very intrusive or noticeable to a typical traveler. Airport security, while much more thorough, is very efficient.

This is all a bit disingenuous. The nation is less wealthy now than it was before the attacks. By mathematical logic and whatever despair that logic produces, there must be some personal sacrifice. Individualism, as a philosophy, recognizes the brutal combination of victimization and personal failure. Bringing Osama bin Laden and his hundreds of minions to justice does not reverse the loss. Yet, compared to the way the country had to respond to Pearl Harbor in 1941, there has been little systematic sacrifice outside of the direct victims of the attacks and their families.

I conjure up images of Jimmy Carter in 1977, when I honestly expected eventual gasoline rationing and energy police. Or Ross Perot, who in his 1992 campaign talked about "shared sacrifice." But during the Reagan, Bush #1 and Clinton years, we seemed to prove that with, less government regulation, we could produce our way out of these problems. Reaganism worked.

And in many ways this may be true again. The technology that we will be forced to develop now for security purposes will eventually provide other benefits that will add wealth. Despite all the layoffs, there are high-paying jobs going begging for qualified people in areas related to security, as well as construction efforts related to infrastructure—highways, bridges, sewers, dams, light rail. This all sounds like an FDR New Deal? I hope that this time around it will be more private, but efforts could be made, for example, to help laid off airline employees work in security areas.

Business needs to pay more attention to substance and less to superficial numbers. I have nothing against day traders (and even short sellers), but we may need some tax law incentives to encourage longer term investment. The scale of corporate fraud and improper accounting at a few large companies such as Enron and WorldCom amounts to a bout of fiscal terrorism. This problem has probably consumed more jobs and personal wealth than did the attacks. The big areas for investment are infrastructure, security, health care and, most of all—and here is the best opportunity—education.

Business will have to pay even more attention to its own security. This could mean more thorough background screening, a practice (as we already know from medical screening) that could invade employee privacy and create discrimination based on ethnicity, lifestyle, or associations. Businesses will have to pay more for physical infrastructure security. Government will have to provide extra assistance in such areas as protecting consolidated disaster recovery centers (for banks and financial institutions) with no-fly zones, to protecting natural gas lines and nuclear power plants. The use of optical backup storage and cables will make systems less vulnerable to electronic pulse attacks.

One area that has received attention is money laundering, the "know your customer" concept noted above. Down the pike, there may eventually be more legal attention (outside of the IRS) paid to whether individual proprietorships (even mine) are operationally self-supporting. Already some wire transfer services, or hawalas, sending money to citizens in poor countries like Somalia with an honor system have been shut down (some have re-opened) because of suspicion of money laundering. I was driven away from a public sidewalk while filming in St Paul by a Somali business owner who feared that I was from the government. Emails offering "Nigerian scams" to collect overseas money abounded in the days after the attacks.

A particular area should also be long-term solutions to controversies over global warming and oil supplies. The evidence is mounting that our continued dependence upon fossil fuels (let alone those from the Middle East) will cause grave political and economic difficulties in the future. Genuine controversy exists not over global warming but over the true remaining reserves of recoverable oil supplies. Industry should gear up for building alternate infrastructures, such as those based upon hydrogen as a fuel. The world may not tolerate our disproportionate use of non-renewable resources.

It is in this area that the entertainment industry and book publishing industry has a civic responsibility for some innovation, to create better customers. Hollywood should divert some effort away from copycat escapist entertainment towards films with real social and educational content.

This is a time for thoughtful investment, not for conspicuous and frivolous consumption. Over the long run as the short, our way of life—personal mobility, lifestyle and expressive choice—is at considerable risk.

Stable companies should consider alternatives to layoffs, like shorter work weeks, reducing executive perks and compensation, and careful tailoring of personnel and professional development policies. When they do lay off employees, they must be fair. Northwest Airlines actually tried to deny some of its employees severance since it claimed its union contract allowed this in national emergencies.

Individualism requires the expectation of personal gain and reward, but individualism also understands the notion of "that's the breaks"—sacrifice is not always evenly distributed, and in the interests of freedom in the long term, perhaps it cannot be. Employees and stakeholders of targeted industries (let alone the direct victims of the attacks) will sacrifice disproportionately, and this is a natural result of risk-taking.

But we also need to bring some balance back into our ideas about individual responsibility, to the idea that sometimes one has to take care of others beside oneself. Family is supposed to accomplish this naturally—and that makes attention to the same-sex marriage and gay parenting issues mandatory, even if doing so makes others uncomfortably self-conscious about their personal values and upon their dependence on the abstract notion of marriage. Coming back full circle, we see how whole generations have lost sight of this—and have come to believe that they can carry out their own lives with no prior obligations. It doesn't work that way, it never did. We need to become aware again of deservedness, of the need to pay your dues.

This might mean going the extra mile on the job when there is no extra compensation for on-call production support, or it might mean expected participation in national community service, not just at age 18 but at various points in one's life. It might even allowing employers to institute the "family wage." It certainly means having employers or shareholders stop paying huge bonuses and parachutes to executives that in today's world seem inappropriately garish (and certainly some of these executives should share in the sacrifice.) We need a mentality where employers and individuals expect to see this, more through spontaneous order than government itself. It won't be easy. But a lot of the middle-class sacrifice in terms of a whole variety of economic losses (beyond the tragedy of those most directly affected by the attacks) has already occurred.

And, yup, I have not always lived up to my own teachings. Perhaps I lived a lot of my adult life in a generation that valued self-expression to the point that it did not require this expression be authenticated by taking care of others. No need for the details here. But for the foreseeable future, whatever opportunity I may find, I will live modestly.

One of my goals would be to participate in setting up a few town halls around the country to examine this axis between civil liberties and public interest. The psychological schism incubated in Western democracies by the paradoxes of the gay world are now transposed into global politics, where the meaning of the individual in relation to God, the state, and particularly to gender is challenged again on a colossal scale. As former Vice President Walter Mondale points out (speech on Nov. 29, 2001), diversity (acting in a society under a rule of law and tempered by responsibility) actually offers a tremendous advantage against an adversary determined to impose conformity, whether in the name of religion, folksiness, hero-worship, mysticism, equality or glory. However, even with an efficient outcome to the war on terrorism, there is every reason to believe that in the future many citizens (especially younger ones) may not enjoy the same degree of individual autonomy that has come to be taken for granted. The idea of social obligations will come back. The ensuing debate does fit the proposals made earlier for "Bill of Rights II". And I would want to capture it in the can—on film.

My optimistic view of a more moral America in *Do Ask Do Tell* (1997) faithfully presents personal freedom increased in conjunction with personal responsibility. The limits on individual choice seemed to come largely from within, the requirements of a society based on "ordered liberty." The circumscription from without seemed to me to be based more on conventionally held ideas about threats to national security. These perils included the deterioration of states in which we knew there were serious problems (nationalism in Russia, communism in North Korea, overthrow of moderate Islamic regimes, more conventional aggression like Saddam Hussein's and the possibility of catastrophic individual terrorist attacks in the McVeigh or Unabomber nature, possibly with weapons of mass destruction).

I knew about the reports about missing biological and suitcase nuclear weapons (from Russia) but did not give them specific attention. I perceived of terrorism as intermittent in nature. Recognition of occasional or unpredictable possibilities led me to argue that problems within the military (such as the dishonest way in which "don't ask, don't tell" had been implemented) could some day have national security consequences.

I have noticed on the logs of this domain (hppub.com) significant access from Islamic countries, especially Saudi Arabia and Malaysia (sometimes Oman, Iran, and other remote countries) and I believed that, despite the filtering in many countries, persons in the Islamic world were reading some of my musings about individualism. These thoughts would offend many elements in their patriarchal culture, at least isolated persons or elements. So I am an infidel with whom, in a global village, there can be no peaceful coexistence!

I had no idea then that an organization like Al Qaeda could be plotting such intricate, nihilistic plots without being more noticed. I did not grasp the idea that a large terrorist organization could essentially take over weak states like Afghanistan and use their substates to launch attacks on or infiltrate Western society with the organization to carry out (through martyrdom) horrific atrocities, even with low tech, high concept approaches.

While a number of journalists had suspected this possibility, I think that the particular combination of detailed planning and innocent technology escaped the radar screens of most authorities, given the political climate. It might be argued that remaining Al Qaeda or other groups intended this approach and still had detailed plans in place to follow up with weapons of mass destruction.

This brings us back to understanding the relationship between Islamic history and the way the Islamic religion seems to have evolved so as to emphasize the importance of obedience to the tribe or group and to the formalities of ritual practice. Fundamentalist Islamic convictions about Western culture are firmly felt but seem incomprehensible to most Westerners. Christianity and Judaism have developed a theological respect for (and even dependence on) individual choice and free will (and this comment applies all the more to conservative denominations such as Mr. Ashcroft's) that is in historical terms rather recent and unique. Indeed, the ability of Christendom to form stable nations and states with a culture advanced enough to separate church and state took centuries to evolve, along with a geography that ultimately encouraged advanced economic growth.

Princeton Professor of Near Eastern Studies Michael Scott Doran gives the complete historical detail of how collectively religious Islamic ideology drove the formation of large terrorist networks and the series of escalating attacks. "On September 11, the attackers undoubtedly imagined themselves to be retracing the Prophet's steps." [62] For a people to take their religion as a complete source of personal identity is perhaps the historical norm, and the West may be the outlier.

Ultimately balancing individual expressive liberty with general welfare and security, even given the shocking nature of the new threats, remains a matter of legal and moral principles. These principles apply even as we recognize that the enemy seems determined to exploit our openness as some kind of destabilizing evil and leverage that freedom against us with unpredictable attacks. When elucidating seemingly new legal principles that allow increased surveillance, restrictions upon expressive association and the use of military justice possibly even with American citizen civilians, we need some convincing and principled way to draw a line. That boundary would involve evidence of the presence of weapons of mass destruction or clear evidence of intention to produce mass violence or destruction for its own sake. (This is not so far from how we used to view the Communist Party, when the legal definition of Communism—with the capital "C" and in comparison to socialism—included promotion of the use of violent conflict or overthrow of the government.)

With free speech concerns, we need to focus upon individual ethics, so that individual speakers know when they really could be endangering others, either through circumstances or negligence such as in allowing personal computers to be used for cyber attacks. We should find a way to draw the line on when speech incites violence or "an imminent threat of lawless action." With social obligations, we need to develop the expectation that there will be some (including service expectation), and that specific kinds of people, like gays and lesbians, will not be excluded. If we do experience sudden overwhelming or repeated attacks (again, radiological or nuclear worry me the most), leading to martial law and breakdown of normal modes of freedom, expression and mobility, people will have not much left but biological family, and it's not a nice prospect to be forced back into that by moralistic external cultures (which themselves do not really exude family values as we understand them).

Every decade since World War II had its distinctive personality along the way to a build-up of individualism and personal liberty. We have reached the crisis and catharsis. We know the theme of the start of the new millennium.

So, can we have a "Bill of Rights II"? Yes, but we must face the gravity of the threats and prove to ourselves that we can contain them. Asymmetric warfare, while it could not conquer a Western country in the conventional sense of overthrowing a government and evicting it from power, could make a free and open society as we know it—so rooted in law and justice and supportive of individual choices—unsustainable. We simply cannot afford to miss any more of these big threats (and this comment may apply to Saddam Hussein). We really do need to look in a structured way to draw the line against weapons of mass destruction with respect to most individual rights issues, including free speech, search and seizure, privacy, criminal due process, immigration, and maybe even national service. We have to learn to determine when we are playing fair with the way we set our own priorities.

(This essay was first posted on hppub.com on Thanksgiving Day, 2001, and it has been maintained up to the time of publication in this book.)

4:

ON ITS FACE, CAN "DON'T ASK, DON'T TELL" REALLY BE CONSTITUTIONAL?

One immediate problem when asked whether the military's "don't ask, don't tell" policy is constitutional, is the definition of "don't ask, don't tell."

The most reasonable definition is the Enclosure on Homosexuality in the Defense Authorization Act of 1993, and the supplementary DOD (2/28/1994) policy that theoretically administers this enclosure. The legislated enclosure requires the discharge of any servicemember who has committed homosexual acts, has stated that he or she is homosexual or bisexual (that is, as defined further in the statute, that he or she may have a "propensity" to engage in actual homosexual acts), or has attempted a same-sex marriage. At face value, this provision includes any statement made to anyone, even family members or civilian friends even when not on active duty. The "marriage" provision seems especially gratuitous since no state recognizes marriage as such, but it is likely that a "civil union" as in Vermont or a homosexual domestic partnership seeking benefits and reasonably believed to be "sexual" would require discharge.

There are legislated exceptions, mainly aimed at false statements ("queen for a day") intentionally made to seek discharge. The policy as administered by the DOD enclosure, however, explicitly allows "associative" behaviors (such as going to gay bars or marching in gay parades in civilian clothes) as not to be construed as statements that indicate a propensity to commit homosexual acts. Until very recently, statements made to military lawyers, medical personnel or chaplains were considered indicative. The policy as legislated in the enclosure does state that the military need not ask sexual orientation unless deemed necessary by later circumstances (ask if necessary). In practice, some commands have been very aggressive in attempting to ferret out homosexuals, attempting to give undesirable discharges, and in "lesbian baiting." They have "negligently" ignored sexual harassment aimed a women or at men perceived to be gay.

In practice, this means that no one can serve in the military indefinitely and live an openly "gay" life. Some servicemembers may be able to enjoy some private gay "social life" when on leave (or at home off-base) and attend gay-sponsored events anonymously but that's about it.

The Congress and the Pentagon attempted, in enacting this 1993 policy, to have it both ways. On paper, the enclosure appears to codify the military ban into law. But the 1994 Clinton administrative policy written by DOD pretends to allow gay servicemembers a zone of privacy as long as they "never talk about it" and are most discreet. The Clinton DOD policy maintains that "sexual orientation" as an abstract preference is not an issue for military service, but that "homosexual conduct," including predictive statements, does constitute grounds for exclusion or discharge.

So can this be constitutional? Article I, Section 8 of the Constitution explicitly gives Congress and the executive branch the power to regulate the military and the conduct of its members. When one considers that the Supreme Court refused (in *Bowers v. Hardwick*, 1986) to declare sodomy laws unconstitutional, one realizes that as a constitutional matter the federal government may certainly control the private sexual lives of servicemembers and make homosexual acts illegal and grounds for discharge.

On September 23, 1998 the Second Circuit upheld the constitutionality of the so-called "Don't Ask, Don't Tell" 1993 law, following the Fourth Circuit in 1996. With three appellate circuits now upholding the law and none striking it down, it appears unlikely at this time that the Supreme Court will consider this issue any time soon. All three circuits have placed particular emphasis on specific powers given in the Constitution to Congress to regulate the military. The Fourth Circuit (in *Thomasson*) actually mentioned an earlier Supreme Court ruling allowing a male-only draft as an example of the tremendous deference given to the military by Article I, Section 8.

Nevertheless, the more recent story of Arizona state representative Steve May is so provocative as to suggest that the policy still could be challenged. May had announced his homosexuality to the state legislature in debating same-sex domestic partner benefits and then was called up by the Army Reserves, where he was an officer in the Engineer Corps. May correctly maintained that he was discharged for statements made when not in military status and not expecting to be called up, but according to DADT his "civilian" behavior is still grounds for discharge. May challenged his discharge order, and the parties finally settled by May's agreeing not to reenlist—an agreement that could have prevented the most serious constitutional challenge yet.

But may the military equate statements with conduct? May it treat homosexuals as a class (and this makes a pretty good pun on object-oriented software) in a pejorative manner compared to heterosexuals?

Up to a point, common law generally allows the concept of **rebuttable presumption** (that certain statements or facts mean that other facts are probably true) to be used when reasonable. Less clear is whether the concept can be used in statutory law (although we see it in examples such as the "no jokes" laws for airport behavior). Certainly the policy will cause verbal or non-verbal statements by homosexuals to be viewed with much more suspicion than corresponding statements by heterosexuals.

There are essentially two major lines of argument to follow:

The simplest argument may be *equal protection*. That is, even granted the legitimacy of the presumption device, government is differentially punishing heterosexual and homosexual servicemembers for relatively the same conduct. (It might also be possible to pose a "relativistic" argument in terms of unconstitutional gender discrimination.)

According to current case law, it is most unlikely that the Court would recognize this argument of "ratios." It will say that all servicemembers have the same rights to heterosexual "conduct" only. However, this could change if scientific evidence of genetic or biological roots of sexual orientation becomes more commonly accepted (as already reported in the writings of Chandler Burr and others).

In general, both legislatures and courts have tended to give gays "quasi-suspect class" status, a concept that works well in civil-rights laws for race (and would apply if the military still tried to discriminate on the basis of race, which in isolated cases it sometimes does). The prohibition of discrimination on the basis of biological gender has resulted in the opening of most military jobs to women (and may even allow women to serve on submarines soon). Sometimes suspect class reasoning is used with respect to religion, which itself is behavior, so there is some basis for claiming that sexual orientation ought to get the same consideration in law.

The other (and I believe more promising) major argument maintains that the DADT policy unacceptably violates the First Amendment, mostly in regard to *free speech* but also freedom of association. First Amendment violations always require strict scrutiny. Now, the government has obviously tried to bypass the First Amendment with its rebuttable presumption clause. When public safety or national security are at stake, presumption is an acceptable (common law) state device to somewhat limit unusually disruptive speech. One can even say that the need for military unit cohesion, good order and discipline are so critical (to life-risking missions) that use of presumption is necessary (and hence we have "deference to the military," a concept probably rooted in an explicit due process exception in the Fifth Amendment).

One possible counter-argument, however, is that Congress has literally redefined the words "gay" and "lesbian" in a federal statute in terms of "propensity to engage in homosexual acts." This device might be unconstitutional if there is a credible public understanding (as established in published literature) that "gay" refers to something more generic, like "psychological surplus" as we have developed in the *Do Ask, Do Tell* book and elsewhere at the hppub.com web site. The credibility of such an argument would depend on general observations of public behavior. For example, the increased willingness of heterosexuals to march in gay events to advance the causes of their organizations (the Libertarian party is one example) tends to undermine the idea that the public views the word "gay" in terms of sexual acts.

But, as hinted above, the (Arizona state representative) Steve May case may well force a complete rethinking of all the precepts used to justify DADT. The "overbroad" application of the rebuttable presumption clause to impute conduct from statements may unacceptably infringe upon the First Amendment (and go beyond the "least restrictive means") when it is so broad as to include statements expected to remain private (outside of military hearsay) or to include public statements made by reservists while not in military status, particularly in the May case by an elected public official with a genuine public policy motive for his speech.

Ironically the Supreme Court, in limiting the government's ability to interfere with "politically incorrect" speech in the *James Dale v. Boy Scouts of America* case (in actually ruling against the liberal "gay" position) may someday have a harder time justifying the military's own intrusion upon the First Amendment now, out of its own neo-conservative values. If the Court were to follow least restrictive means analysis in a manner consistent with other First Amendment cases, the military could find itself in a position of having to allow gays whose statements had been made while not in military status (and when not expecting to be called up) to serve. It would then have to come up with a legitimate code of conduct such as had been proposed by Rand in 1993,[63] for all servicemembers, reservists or permanent parties. There would be no legitimate reason that it could not allow all gays who comply with the same code to serve. So the whole policy could fall to a kind of *reducto ad absurdum*.

There are other possible arguments, such as appeals to international law. In fact, since the European Court ruled on the matter in 1999, Britain has been forced to drop its own version of "Don't Ask, Don't Tell" for a Rand-style code of conduct. Only Greece and Turkey, among NATO allies, now maintain a military gay ban, so the United States is withdrawing into a position where it can justify its policy, when compared to allies, only by maintaining that only the U.S. is macho enough to do the real fighting, a position that seems insulting to our crucial allies.

Even if the Supreme Court were to allow most of the "Don't Ask, Don't Tell" policy to stand, it may, however, strike down exceptions which allow military officers to escape accountability for illegal investigations, and require that servicemembers improperly discharged be compensated and be given full retirement benefits.

WHO CARES?

Why should the average American, especially the non-gay civilian, care about this issue? There are two approaches to answering this.

Some of the legal artifacts of the policy mean that it can involve civilians. Most gays in the military do not find out that they are homosexual until they are in the service. Any servicemember who announces homosexual orientation to anyone, including any civilian friend or family member, may be discharged, and in some cases military investigators have actually sought information from civilians. The military provides a viable way to pay for college education and even graduate, medical or law school for persons (often women or minority members) otherwise unable to afford it, and yet the military has sometimes pursued recoupment of scholarship monies from persons that it discovers to be gay.

The Pentagon has (through the 1996 Solomon Amendment, now partially repealed) stiff-armed colleges and law schools into allowing military recruiters on campus in direct violation of non-discrimination policies of these institutions and sometimes in violation of state laws. Some jobs require membership in the reserves or considerable previous experience in uniform (or the ability to relate to military members as customers), or may rely on skills usually learned in the military (such as the case for commercial airline pilots and even many aircraft mechanics). The ban may thus contribute to indirect discrimination in the civilian job market.

Until a decade or so ago, it was difficult for gays to get security clearances even in civilian employment. Now, however, both the FBI and CIA seem willing to accept open gays (that is, homosexuals who do not hide their sexual orientation and conceivably make themselves blackmail targets), and often work in these agencies involves living in quasi-military environments (such as the FBI Academy in Quantico or in primitive overseas duty stations). A new department of Homeland Security in response to terrorism would have uniformed (Coast Guard, National Guard) components working together with civilian law enforcement and intelligence, and these observations weaken the claim that the presence of gays undermines unit cohesion or sense of propriety in forced intimacy.

But there is a more personal side to how I would answer this, as related in detail in the first *Do Ask, Do Tell* book. In 1961, during the Cold War, I was thrown out of a civilian college (William and Mary) for telling the Dean of Men that I perceived myself as homosexual. The reasoning used by the college in those days sounded a lot like the military's reasons (sexual privacy) for trying or pretending to keep out gays today. In the ensuing months, I actually underwent inpatient therapy at National Institutes of Health, and the mildly reparative therapy of that Cold War era seemed determined that every man fulfill his "heterosexual obligation" before taking any other part in society.

To avoid besmirching my reputation I took the draft physical three times until I actually served in the Army during the Vietnam years without incident. But there has still been a practical effect on my career (in information systems) of minimizing involvement even as a civilian with the military. Today, the ban seems profoundly insulting; it implies that because of my intimate choices (and no matter how discreet, private and careful my behavior) I somehow burden society, particularly in the task of defending the country.

I grew up during an era when there was a draft, and when there was an assumption that young men, at least, had a responsibility to take their turn offering themselves to protect others (particularly women and children) before they had lives of their own. A certain social context and a sense of limitation circumscribed the choices people could make with their lives, as many men even today do especially dangerous work.[64] Even today, the military sometimes has difficulty meeting its recruiting goals with acceptable people, and there are calls for other kinds of national service that would require young adults to live in close quarters in quasi-military situations. Some commentators, such as Charles Moskos at Northwestern University (who had helped author "don't ask don't tell" in 1993) have called for reinstating the draft in the wake of the 9-11 attacks, a possibility that we consider in more detail in another chapter.

Some conservatives have suggested that "don't ask, don't tell" be abandoned and replaced with "must ask, must tell" (essentially the case from 1981 until 1993; during the Vietnam war the services and draft boards did not ask after 1965). As unsatisfactory as is "don't ask, don't tell," going back to "asking" would publicly confirm that the government has a warrant to probe into the most intimate parts of a person's life and to regulate intimate personal choices. (In fact, SLDN recently reported that the Air Force Reserve has been "illegally" asking at enlistment ever since the implementation of "don't ask, don't tell.")

Conceivably, government could some day (say, for a prolonged war with Iraq) reinstitute a draft and, given all the progress of the past forty years, renew the shocking practice of identifying young homosexual men (who might at first relish the idea of "telling" to escape a draft). It would set an example that could repeated in other areas, such as teaching and law enforcement (where anti-gay exclusion used to be common). Were such a measure to be legally driven by Congress, it could again jeopardize security clearances for gay civilians and jeopardize fair employment practices of companies that deal with the military. Most of all, it would be profoundly insulting even if Congress tried to offset asking by explicit protections of gays in civilian areas.

The notion of mandatory asking does have precedent in other areas. For example, a handful of states have had regulations requiring asking of sexual orientation for adoptive parents (although now, thankfully the trend is to challenge anti-gay adoption bans in some states, such as Florida). The practice of "asking" about sexual activity (and particularly male homosexual activities since 1977) has long been accepted in blood donations (since there is a theoretical chance that the HIV and perhaps Hepatitis C tests will not find all infected donors), although some medical commentators believe that this is now unnecessary and see it, again, as an insult to gay men. In civilian intelligence employment asking seems to be necessary, and it is apparently not much abused.

The idea of rebuttable presumption has applications in many other areas, such as conflict of interest, where a potential customer is entitled to presume that a professional may compromise his best interests because of temptations for gains from competing sources.

The "don't ask, don't tell" policy seems to have abetted sexual harassment of female servicemembers (lesbian baiting) and in some cases antigay violence. The most tragic recent example was the murder of Barry Winchell in his barracks at Fort Campbell, KY in July 1999. PFC Winchell's mother, Patricia Kutteles, has spoken passionately about this issue, including at the SLDN "Red White and Blue" Party at the Casa de la Vista on Treasure Island in San Francisco Bay on a beautiful October Sunday in 2000, complete with a Navy Blue Angels air show. The policy was the target of the sensational play *Another American: Asking and Telling*,[65] performed by Marc Wolf throughout much of 2000 and 2001.

STATUS AFTER 9-11

Early in the deployments to Afghanistan and other areas associated with the new war on terrorism, the military services, one by one, have announced stop-loss policies to reduce discharges for various reasons. But, at least officially, the services have refused to modify the "don't ask don't tell" policy. "Homosexual conduct" as defined in the 1993 statute still remains grounds for discharge. But there have been practically no news reports of incidents involving homosexual conduct or discharges in areas of deployment. Certainly, gay servicemembers are serving honorably and courageously in the new war on terror, especially in the primitive areas that have been targeted as terrorist hideouts. Most gay discharges seem to take place in stateside commands.

Servicemembers' Legal Defense Network (SLDN) has reported, in its Eight Annual Report,[66] that gay discharges numbered 1250 in 2001, about double the number in 1994, and that the number of harassment complaints was 1075, several times the number in 1994. Anecdotally, however, some servicemembers tell me that many commands pretty much ignore the ban and that a majority of discharges come from straight soldiers wanting to get out of the military. Furthermore, both the Pentagon and Congress have failed to respond to a recommendation by a panel (convened by Judge Walter Cox) in 2000 to rescind the military sodomy laws, as provided in the Uniform Code of Military Justice.

The irony of all of this is that the military probably played a major role in catalyzing the modern gay liberation movement at the end of the 1960s. First, the Cold War provided a public reason for nerds or for men (and women) who would contribute to national security in ways outside of their conventional gender roles (and recall the controversy over student deferments). Then, just after the apex of the 1960s Civil Rights movement, the Vietnam-era draft put men of all kinds of backgrounds and cultures together, and the resentment of the war made homosexuality come across as a cool way to "non-conform" and protest. In the late 1960s, the military was sometimes a better place for gays than a lot of civilian life.

Our president said that terrorists simply "hate those who are not like them." In the military especially there is a minority of members who hate gays as an immune response, as "not like them," and who see their presence as contagious and threatening to their masculinity (just as radical Islam sees Jews and sometimes even all Americans). On Tuesday nights, before enjoying *Queer as Folk* (with its own family values) at the local video bar here in Minneapolis (the Boom), I usually watch *Smallville*, a series that is now a darling of the religious right because it shows a perfect American family with a perfect, role-model teenage boy—the only problem being that to be a perfect kid he needs to be biologically different, preferably born on another planet and "adopted."

In one episode, extraterrestrial Clark Kent yearns to be "normal" but soon realizes he is better off if he has his powers (like his "speed") back, even though that "superman" capacity makes him "different" and hampers his fitting in with other young men (being allowed to play high school football, for example). His adoptive father repeatedly counsels him not to disclose fully who he is. It's just too much for others to live with.[67] Well, if he goes to a military service academy next year, he'd better not tell Sam Nunn.

5:

OUR NEW DEBATE ON NATIONAL SERVICE AND THE DRAFT

Since the terrorist attacks last September (2001), Charles Moskos (a sociology professor and chairman at Northwestern University) has authored several stimulating pieces regarding his case for resuming the draft and about the renewed interest in national or public service and volunteerism. In the November 2001 *Washington Monthly* with "Now Do You Believe We Need a Draft" (and in the November 4, 2001 *Washington Post*) Dr. Moskos openly argued that young Americans were not, contrary to media perception, readily volunteering to join the military. He also claimed that an overwhelming additional need exists for people to fill new domestic security positions, such as at airports, borders or nuclear power plants.

In the Spring 2002 *The Public Interest*, Moskos, with "Reviving the Citizen-Soldier," confronted the civilian reader with the need to accept increased military casualties and emphasized the case for short-term enlistments. In all cases he has stressed the ukase to induce youths from more privileged social classes to serve. For example, he proposed in the *Public Interest* article, "Bring back a draft that starts conscription at the top of the social ladder or establish recruitment appeals that will garner some share of privileged youth." The December 2001 *American Enterprise* published a counterpoint between Charles Moskos and

Lawrence Korb on draft proposals, and in that debate Moskos took the position that the draft could remain male-only.

On September 14, 2001, immediately following the major terrorist assault on New York and Washington, the Chairman of the Senate Armed Services Committee Carl Levin (D-Michigan) suggested on CNN that the military draft should be reinstituted. According to a CNN poll that tragic week, 66% of Americans favored resumption of the draft if necessary to combat asymmetric terrorist warfare. However the Pentagon has consistently maintained some distance from such a proposal.[68] On September 19, 2001, White House spokesman Ari Fleisher stated, "There is no consideration of…(reinstating the draft)…at this time, and from my conversations with the Pentagon, it's not something they anticipate." On September 25, 2001, Secretary of Defense Donald Rumsfeld said at a Pentagon news conference, "(The draft)…is not something that we've addressed and it is not something that is immediately before us. At the moment I do not foresee the need to do that." Tim Cavanaugh made light of draft resumption cries in a whimsical missive in the February 2002 *Reason*.[69] Libertarians generally comment that conscripts would tend to become dead weight, needing to be supported and nannied.

There have been other recent suggestions for the draft, often with an option of alternative civilian national service. For example, on the December 31, 2001 "News Hour with Jim Lehrer" on Public Broadcasting, Robin Gerber from the University of Maryland advocated a mandatory national service obligation to be fulfilled some time between the ages of 18 and 24. In "Hot Careers in a Cool Market: Ask Not What Business Can Do for You; Ask What You Can Do for Business," Jim Thompson and Mike Woodward wrote that employees with computer data encryption skills tend to be young and of draft age, and that companies now worry that key people "could one day be called up by the military," apparently even if not already in the Guard, the Reserves or from ROTC programs. This comment is an open admission that an expectation that the draft (as well as more reserve call-ups) might be resumed during the war on terrorism is now being taken seriously by some employers.[70] On September 23, 2001, Vance Opperman, writing for the *Minneapolis Star Tribune*, suggested that middle-aged people be drafted for homeland security duties. The Supreme Court has accepted the idea that a draft is constitutional even when male-only (such as *Rostker v. Goldberg*, 1981).

My own drilling into the facts about the practical need (let alone philosophical acceptability) for a draft or other compulsory service would raise serious questions. For example, the Transportation Security Administration published job qualifications for new better-paid airport security professionals, and one requirement (beyond a clean background investigation and citizenship) would be at least a year in security experience or practical work with screening or X-ray equipment. They really don't need "everybody." [However, as of August 2002 the TSA was allowing that a high school diploma can substitute for security experience, for Transportation Security Screeners and even for Lead Transportation Security Screeners.[71] Of course, the employment screening process prefers specific security experience, and the training program to follow is very rigorous, regimented and unforgiving of small lapses in attention to detail.[72]]

But the government has for decades nurtured rather covert programs to train lay person "civilian reservists" for emergency duty in the wake of unexpected domestic disaster. Security in any conceivable vulnerable area, ranging from border patrols to radiological substance detection and to Internet worms and viruses requires trained, dedicated, well-compensated professionals.

Since American society has gradually become more individualistic, today's younger adult generation tends away from awareness of the possibility of a draft even though draft registration cards (for 18-25 year-old males) are offered conspicuously today in United States post offices. Nixon stopped the active draft in 1973; there was some discussion of resuming it during the Carter administration when the Soviet Union invaded Afghanistan at the end of 1979 (the legal warrant for Congress or president to enact it was restored), but otherwise there was little public attention to future military conscription until the terrorist attacks. As Shanker pointed out, an earlier military service act has expired and Congress would again have to authorize resuming the draft.

In fact, however, the Selective Service System (http://www.sss.gov) has remained in business, and is quite open to answering questions from the general public. For example, the Selective Service office in Arlington, VA shared with me a 1994 memo from the Clinton administration that a contingent authority to draft was still needed because the military services could find themselves suddenly without sufficient medical personnel—an idea reinforced now by concerns about bioterrorism. Another area of severe shortage is military personnel, particularly in special forces, with fluency in non-European languages.

During the Vietnam era the personal risk of military service was a controversial issue for draftees. Student deferments were available for several years (until a lottery was instituted) and these became a source of political and moral discontent. Persons with technical education generally could get Military Occupational Specialties with less combat risk, often (as in my case) even if drafted. At earlier times (until Vietnam escalated in 1965) married fathers and even married men without children could be deferred ("Kennedy fathers" and "Kennedy husbands").

One point of interest to me is that the Moskos pieces do not refer the earlier controversy about gays in the military. Moskos had made himself a major architect of the "don't ask don't tell" policy adopted in 1993 and 1994 regarding homosexuals in the military. For eight years, the Servicemembers Legal Defense Network (SLDN), a legal services organization that I have supported, has helped uniformed servicemembers chased by misdirected or bad-faith enforcement of this policy by the Armed Forces.

The "military gay ban" is a convoluted topic, still worthy of a separate detailed treatment in public policy journals, but in the context of discussions about a draft, two observations are important. First, the policy may be interpreted now as an insult or a source of shame for gay men in particular, because it insinuates that gay men burden the country and cannot (as a matter of law, almost) pay their dues (as potential "citizen-soldiers") with regard to citizenship and therefore would cheat the system. Second, if the draft were re-implemented, there would be temptation by government and associated industries to use it to justify new discrimination against gays, men especially.

Personally, I rather pooh-pooh the idea that people would "get away" with "coming out" to avoid being drafted. I raised this issue with Moskos last November in a private email, and he wrote back, incredibly, "Gays must come out for conscription. Then the ban would be lifted." Other national service programs (which obviously might become "choices" in lieu of the Armed Forces) such as the Peace Corps do not exclude gays, although the practical circumstances of service (particularly in underdeveloped countries) often may require a "don't ask don't tell" paradigm for deportment.[73]

My own personal history becomes relevant now. I was booted out of the College of William and Mary in 1961 for telling the Dean of Men that I thought that I was gay, and the reasoning used to justify my "medical" dismissal was the same that Sam Nunn and Charles Moskos articulated about gays in the barracks during the 1993 debates. Expecting blackballing and discrimination during this post-McCarthy, Cold War era, I managed to recover from this setback, graduated from another college and graduate school, and actually served in the Army from 1968-1970 without incident after "volunteering for the draft." I was "sheltered" during my service and avoided Vietnam. While other inductees speculated about "getting infantry," I recall a day in Basic Training when a sergeant called out, regarding my application for a particular MOS, "Hey, you missed a college grad."

Conservative publications have stimulated intermittent discussions about the limits of "self-ownership." During the stock market insider trading scandals of the late 1980s (long before Enron and Anderson) some commentators called for mandatory national service as a way to teach young adults ethics in an otherwise brutally competitive society. In recent years we have anticipated a crisis in custodial eldercare, as families become smaller, adult children move away and nursing homes become overwhelmed with elderly persons no longer able to fend for themselves. These examples underscore the renewed assertion that practical social obligations, not just those related to military service, go along with life's freely chosen paths. Perhaps the past couple of generations, even mine, have gotten off easy.

6:

A Temperate View of Gay Conservatism: Is "Gay Conservative" an Oxymoron?

Well, I'll confess. I'm a *gaycon*. That's *The Nation*'s term for a new kind of alien, the gay conservative. I've always felt that I was looking at my world from an off-center perspective and that experience gives me an unusual way to understand things. But maybe that viewpoint works to my personal advantage. My method of "attack" was peaceful enough, to self-publish a controversial book and follow with a supporting web site.

The best way to develop my brand of gay conservatism, which blends with libertarianism, is to use autobiographical induction. I would say that I am a *neo-conservative* in that I don't believe that government should get involved in making personal moral choices for people or should achieve social justice with merely group-based remedies (like affirmative action preferences), but that serious "moral questions" about the way we authenticate our personal choices with responsibility keep growing and need to be on the table of our public debate. We must not take our freedoms for granted.

I did grow up in the Cold War years as a rather sissy boy who made up for lacking masculinity with nerdy academics. The teasing and taunts were not as severe as what other gay kids report, but they were sometimes enough for me to want to switch from playing chicken to lashing back. Once I actually fought with fingernails; and using an immature teenager's reasoning, I teased another student for having an epileptic seizure in class.

I interpreted the taunts as the other boys' maintaining that I would be a burden. Once I was called "lazybones" at a day camp. Men were supposed to support women and children. A "girlish" boy who just got good grades would cheat the system. This way of looking at my problems would shape my political and social views for the rest of my life. I probably did not fully understand that much of this aggressive bullying behavior related to the boys' trying to achieve social power among their own peers. Yet, I found myself attracted to men who had a particular combination of qualities that I coveted. Homosexual attraction was narcissistic, but that juvenile aspect made it suit my psychological purposes. Homosexuality seemed like a reaction to a social projection that there was one right way to act and particularly to look like a man.

I was kicked out of the College of William and Mary right after Thanksgiving my freshman semester in 1961 for telling the Dean of Men that I considered myself a "latent homosexual." After a stint of mildly reparative therapy at the National Institutes of Health I went to college while living at home, and I went back pretty much into the closet. After graduate school I "volunteered" for the draft in 1968 (I took the physical three times to get past the "psychiatric" issues, while migrating from 4-F to 1-A) and served two years without incident, without going to Vietnam. In the barracks everyone realized that I was gay, but with many of the guys homosexuality was almost a cool mode of passive protest given the attitudes towards Vietnam.

In the 1970s, particularly post-Watergate, I encountered support for the idea that my own private choices and personal fulfillment with others were my own business. As we came out of the worst of the energy and financial crises, people seemed freer to map out their own courses in life, however quietly.

In the 1980s the support for this idea of private choice was seriously threatened by the sudden geometric explosion of the AIDS epidemic. Right wing moral majority demagogues could pontificate that gays threatened and burdened the health and welfare of everyone with their private behaviors. Publicly, the gay community seemed to be gaining new political visibility as a victimized population but the community mounted tremendous volunteer efforts and buddy programs to help persons with AIDS and provided educational outreach that reduced high risk behaviors, especially among younger men. In the meantime, however, the Reagan culture, for all the public moralizing and claims of social conservatism, seemed to be sending new messages to people to "do your own thing." Deregulation of business produced hostile takeovers, instability and layoffs but it encouraged more entrepreneurial activity. People fended more for themselves and singles made decisions, like home-buying, that in the past had generally been made only by families.

Individualism and self-expression would get another big boost as the Internet was made available to the public shortly after a publicly successful military victory in the Persian Gulf. These developments would help set up the somewhat false boom and stock market bubble for the Clinton years. Nevertheless, gay issues would come back to center stage with new debates and public battles (often in court) over gays in the military, gay marriage and parenting, as well as more familiar advocacy of hate crimes protection and of employment discrimination protection.

I entered the debate on the military gay ban by working with a minister who had contact with the White House. I quickly noticed the parallel between arguments by Senator Sam Nunn to keep the ban—"privacy" in the barracks for straight soldiers—and the reasons given by William and Mary thirty years before in kicking me out of school. At the same time, proponents of lifting the ban articulated overly facile arguments similar to those used by Truman to integrate the military racially a half-century before. I saw the policy then in terms of private choice, so a "humane" kind of "don't ask don't tell" policy like what President Clinton first

announced then (1993) seemed like an acceptable or "honorable" compromise.

At the same time, the economic dislocations in the few years before
Clinton took office had particularly drawn attention to the stress on traditional families that the new individually competitive paradigms for the
workplace had promoted. It was often a short-term economic advantage
to be single and have no responsibilities for others. The religious right
could credibly argue that it was traditional families and parents, not gays
and singles with their supposedly cushy disposable incomes and capability of lowballing the workplace, who faced discrimination and who tended
to experience more sacrifice in hard times. Given this situation, visible gay
marriages (if legalized) and gay parents could establish the idea that gays
and lesbians were capable of monogamy, fidelity, and having the responsibility to raise children was well as to care for elderly relatives.

By the mid 1990s, the intellectual case for gay libertarianism as promoted by Gays and Lesbians for Individual Liberty (which would later
enter the *James Dale v. Boy Scouts of America* case by arguing for the Boy
Scouts' freedom of expressive association as a private organization) was
reasonably well known. I would edit GLIL's newsletter, *The Quill*, and
write much of its content then. Libertarianism emphasizes the idea of self-
ownership and total responsibility for one's own actions, as well as great
(*laissez-faire*) reduction on government intervention in both economic
and social areas. For younger well-educated gays who are personally successful in competing on their own, this is a very appealing ideology. On
the other hand, conservatism seems to emphasize economic liberties with
maintenance of government social controls, but with neo-conservatism
respect for liberty gets more complicated in its concern with moral limits
and runs a continuum all the way to libertarianism.

What's wrong with an objectivist political philosophy based on the simple idea of total individual accountability? Well, it's brutal. It can leave
people who stumble in a winner-take-all world that does not accept vic-
timhood as an excuse for failure out in the cold. And fault ranges from

personal failure and lack of initiative, to be sure, to circumstances beyond one's control. Complications may range from corporate misconduct and terrorism to, yes, old-fashioned discrimination based on race, religion, gender and apparent sexual orientation.

That observation supports the conservatives' notion of "family values"—that is, that self-concept and achievement, as well as "sexual aesthetics," should be mediated by strong emotional ties to (biological) family, which will provide a consistent environment in which one is needed and a support structure when one's luck goes south. The trend for young women to postpone maternity for education and career comes under particular criticism.

The other main pillar of conservative thought about the family, articulated much more recently, concerns marriage and the family as a collective social institution, important for children in a way that transcends merely summarizing the effects of individual behaviors. Arguments are advanced that adults are bargaining their own wishes against those the "human resource" of the next generation, and that children are always better off in two-parent legally married (heterosexual) households regardless of the possibility that single parents and gay couples might help reduce the number of orphaned children.

As with excluding gays from the military on unit cohesion grounds, there is no way for government to intentionally favor legally married adults without implying that gays and lesbians are second-class citizens on the basis of their erotic (putatively immoral in the minds of some) inclinations or emotional makeup. One is left with saying that gays and lesbians need to distinguish themselves as individuals (an idea that has been celebrated over the past twenty or so years) but then that comes back as self-indulgent or harmful to families. Letting this one slide would be tantamount to accepting psychological segregation. It is becoming apparent that a moral paradigm of individual responsibility, understood as including responsibility for supporting others but with a diverse choice

of commitments, is the only "logical" way out. "Mathematical" philosophy can be merciless.

Traditional liberals quite correctly criticize the use of family as a purported social equalizer (or guarantor of the welfare of children) on the
grounds that family tends to propagate undeserved wealth and provides a
safe place for non-achievers to hide. And the general nature of liberal strategy has been to classify people into groups or "peoples" and collectively
bargain their rights or entitlements, publicly appearing to reconcile past
and current oppression or discrimination but often bartering for political
favors that still help the entrenched and powerful special interests. The
side effects of such strategy (as with affirmative action preferences) may
include egregious injustice in individual cases. Of course, taken as a
whole, history, even to the most cursory observer, often deals mostly with
peoples as nationalities, religious groups, or races, so political processes
will be tempted to treat gays and lesbians as a people too.

The Nation's article (July 1, 2002) by Richard Goldstein[74] discusses
gays and lesbians as a people in liberal parlance, sometimes united by historical pariah status. (An earlier piece in *The Advocate* [April 2002][75] had
narrowly focused upon gay Republican politicians.) But today the gay
community is a people in the sense that the mockingbird's mimics make
a song. The gay world implements the competitive values of a larger cap-
italist societies. True, gaycons talk about assimilation, but this is more a
way of embracing mainstream values of appeal and achievement.

Both meritocracy and diversity thrive within the homosexual community, often in unconventional ways, as those gays without mouths to feed
may find the usual idea of corporate advancement to be a silly, actually
self-effacing beauty pageant. Drag queens and shaved-chest preppies at
circuit parties can achieve public respect as well as men with more con-
formist (and, for some people, desirable) appearance. This was even true
at the time (1969) of Stonewall, as a very fine film (1996) by that name
demonstrates when a "masculine gay"" helps his effeminate friend get out
of the draft.

It is true that the gay community achieves unity particularly through challenging the political promotion of patriarchal gender roles for social control, but now a similar process is shared by much of mainstream straight America. What is more remarkable about the gay community is how the emphasis has shifted from defending privacy to the idea (especially in the Internet age) of homosexuality as a major component of one's public identity and public self-expression. What can cut deeper than expressing publicly what is important in other people? This expression threatens the psychological comfort and not just religious faith but also sexual identity of individuals who grew up and became dependent on patriarchal values. In a similar way, American society, through its public commercial and global outreach, threatens the "masculinity" of many young men in some Muslim areas of the world, an observation that explains the ferocity of the new asymmetric terrorist threat.

The liberal solutions for gay equality today focus largely upon hate crimes laws and ENDA (Employment Nondiscrimination Act) because these practical remedies seem to be most achievable. Although I might disagree with Log Cabin's reported assertion that ENDA would be unnecessary, I would fear that these milestones would be achieved and that then we would stop. Then we would only feed the notion further that gays and lesbians freeload and cheat the system. Military service, marriage and parenting—all much tougher areas in which to make solid permanent gains—all involve the sacrifice of taking responsibility for others as a component of responsibility for oneself.

The president lectured an Ohio commencement, "A person without responsibility for others is a person who is truly alone." Yet being left alone and without such responsibility seems to have been a large part of the achievement of the gay rights movement until at least the mid 1980s. Neo-conservative writer Jonathan Rauch wrote that his biggest fear was that gays would win marriage rights and then not use them, and this speculation fits into the refusal of many conservatives to take these "equal responsibility" proposals seriously. Homosexual narcissism mocks the institution of marriage, social conservatives say; "women tame men" and only the entire courtship and marital process makes it possible for men, as an end stage of growing up, to channel adolescent sexual and aesthetic energies into bonding with children as parents. It would be the responsibility of neo-progressives (liberal or not) to break this line of circular reasoning with examples from personal experience. Gay neo-conservatives have claimed some minimal success in these responsibility areas, as with the recent passage of the Mychal Judge Act allowing police officers and firemen to name beneficiaries (including domestic partners) should these emergency warriors die in the line of duty (as on 9/11).

The events since September 11, 2001 especially underscore the notion that we really can fail and lose all of our freedoms. Therefore in a democracy we maintain an awareness of the idea of "shared sacrifice" (as Ross Perot called it in 1992) and the possibility that extra demands or intrusions upon personal liberty may be necessary for public safety. A paradox about our individualism is that we are all so interdependent and vulnerable to extreme disruption or worse from criminals, con-artists, and particularly cultural enemies, who see our "accomplishments" as tainted fruits of godlessness or hedonism.

Some moralists, implying that capitalists are "parasites," see the answer to this dichotomy in survivalism or in communitarian personal values that stress meeting the practical needs of other people (perhaps through a mentality of "paying your dues" or menial labor as in a Maoist cultural revolution) instead of self-expression. Younger adults often do not relate to the time when we had conscription and accepted the idea that people (men, at least) owed some kind of service—perhaps intermittently throughout life and not just during young adulthood—to earn the full rights of citizenship and participation; a whole "yuppie" generation (myself included) seems to have gotten away with something (although the legal issues around military service, marriage and parenting have tended to send a message to gays to just opt out of responsibility and do their own things).

A new dimension to the need for service will be the growing eldercare crisis, when the labor for custodial care cannot always be bought. A somewhat voluntary value system that incorporates responsibility for others (paying your dues) as an important public policy objective may be part of the solution. Retreating from capitalism and freedom would lead to a Soviet-style society with all its stagnation, but it is fair to ask why a modern somewhat socialistic society of the Scandinavian model cannot balance liberty with security and public welfare in a manner respectful to gays and lesbians.

In a political scenario where sacrifices are expected, it is tempting to demand more of those with fewer responsibilities or dependents. Nevertheless, liberal social policies in European countries, while having to deal with limits and personal side effects of socializing services like health care, have been able to recognize the need for service and personal commitment and, compared to the United States, often include gays and lesbians as individuals quite capable of military service and family responsibilities.

In the United States, where the social climate still resists the challenge from gays and lesbians to biological family and perhaps to patriarchy, gays and lesbians have sometimes welcomed the calls for less government interference in their abilities to fend for themselves, compete and contribute. Even in areas like health care, gays and lesbians, like the mainstream, wonder whether a stronger public safety net, as with a single-payer system, would sometimes mean that people would not get the cutting-edge new medical treatments when they need them or give the government excuses to monitor private behaviors. The challenge for gay and lesbian people, as part of a larger mainstream, is to take as much personal responsibility as possible and preserve as much individual opportunity as possible.

Since the Civil Rights movement of the 1960s and the Vietnam fiasco, the baby boomer generation has come to embrace a core belief in self-ownership. This concept means that each person, regardless of gender, race, national or religious heritage, or sexual orientation, ought to define his or her own place in the world in ways that make the "singleton" person count. The previous generations had understood freedom in the "context factory" of familial, national and particularly religious ties, which had provided a set of moral and social orders that seemed beyond question as necessary for public welfare as a whole. Most of these ukases had revolved around the family and had accepted the notion of an assigned station or role in life.

Now freedom, when understood as self-ownership and personal autonomy, would need (to borrow from Denish D'Souza) "authentication,"[76] because so much of what seems like legitimate individual self-expression and actualization only makes sense in the context factory of an interdependent technological society that has required sacrifice to build. We are freer to be ourselves because we are richer, and that last assumption is now heavily stressed. *The deepest moral problems seem to center upon reconciling personal expressive choice with meeting the real needs of others, particularly when commitment and opportunity costs are required to meet these specific needs.* Committed family provides both a source of support when people cannot compete and a practical limit on the competitive options for those who care for them. On the other hand, severe economic downturns tend to weed out persons who have overvalued their own ends.

Gay men and lesbians can relate this moral dilemma to the sexual realm. The moral compass of straight society used to revolve around encouraging people to outgrow their differential fantasies and channel their deepest personal energies and expressive purposes into courtship, parenting and durable real-life intimacy, a process that used to be called *aesthetic realism* but that the gay person sees as a total denial of inner identity.

Conservative thought does well when it insists, particularly in a world in which the liberal notions of freedom are challenged by "religious" or other collectivist indignation, that people be held, one by one, accountable for the results of their own choices, particularly when these results are combined in a context of taking care of others beside themselves. But such thought troubles me when it ties moral accountability so closely to one's most intimate emotional choices and to a willingness to tie these choices to procreation. Talk of personal responsibility can anger real victims of injustice by blaming them.

There is much that gay and lesbian culture can contribute to fighting the new challenges to freedom when this culture sees its contribution in terms of individual rights rather than as derived from its status as a community. But this all requires a lot of talk, debate, and a willingness to learn how others think and see things, particularly in a society that may well become less open in order to protect itself and in trying to make everyone pay their dues. I lived through a time when my difference turned into an excuse to escape responsibility for others, and this has come back after all as deadwire "liberation" and recognition of inferior station. This is a time for "do ask, do tell."

7:

NARCISSISM, AFFILIATION AND POLARITY

The most intense and romantic human relationships occur because each partner finds in the other a confirmation of his own personal values. A person feels **affiliation** with the traits and character of the person he loves or who loves him.

The feminine personality[77] experiences affiliation in a manner similar to a sports fan: "we win, they lose." He feels enlarged by being part of a person whom he idealizes, who somehow extends him. He becomes like a company that benefits from being acquired. We could call this process **upward affiliation.**

The masculine personality experiences affiliation by possessing someone who loves him and who gives him value, and more confidence in his own independent self as a moral motivator of others. We could call this **possessive affiliation.**

Sometimes this process goes a little further. The feminine personality may covet the qualities of his ideal to the extent that he wishes to be like the ideal. In a similar way, the masculine personality may want the feeling qualities of his beloved to become integrated into the processes of his own personality. We call this process **narcissism.** The narcissist attempts a kind of face-off, and sometimes approaches relations with favored others with a lot of histrionics and infatuation.

Narcissism is generally perceived to be a gay-male phenomenon, with great negativity. It's the sugar-daddy-bald-legged-old-man-and-handsome stud (Wilde-Bosie) syndrome. Erich Fromm in "The Art of Loving" compared it to **symbiosis**. But actually its main appearance is in the conventional heterosexual world in what George Gilder called "the sexual princess problem," something that drives the divorce rate. Narcissism, at its worst, can grow to be very destructive. Criminologists tend to associate it with a kind of sociopathy in which a person exhibits a totally unrealistic apperception of his own importance, and then engages in such anti-social behaviors as stalking, murder (along the "O.J." pattern—"if I can't have you, nobody else can"), or even terrorism. More commonly, the narcissist will notice a certain emptiness in his relations with ordinary people around him. He doesn't really care (in the sense of inner excitement and willingness to prioritize) about someone whose appearance doesn't turn him on. This emphatically does not mean he expects sex or even physical intimacy with someone who attracts him, but it does make him critical of someone who does not.

In traditional heterosexual marriage, there is a convenient opportunity to outgrow the affiliation and even outright narcissism that made the couple fall in love in the first place. That is, beget and raise children. Parenting gives a couple something to do to build a relationship like nothing else. But in some marriages and in most gay couples, both partners need to exercise continuous creativity in the love and power dichotomy to outgrow initial romantic infatuation.

A greater problem occurs when a relationship starts where one partner is narcissistic and the other is not. It is very difficult to maintain momentum in such couplings, beyond platonic friendship; and even that can fail if the "superior" partner perceives the other's offering as a fake, or if the other appears to feel ashamed of or guilty about his intentions. The narcissist finds himself in a position of expecting a "quality" from another Mr.

Right that he cannot, either due to factors beyond his control or due to a laziness defect deep within his character, match. He then finds settling for something more "realistic" as motivated by just not being alone, and finally he must choose between remaining alone on his "road less traveled" or settling into some kind of ascetic or charitable spiritual or religious discipline.

This whole imbalance issue reminds one of the unspoken social ukase, to allow one's innermost feelings and drives to be molded by others into a practical, balanced, but deepening sexuality that keeps one alive and in touch with the real needs of others. After all, many marriages and partnerships form and last with very little affiliation, let alone narcissism. We call this societal expectation **aesthetic realism**, as it was known in the 1970s.

Of course, it is incorrect to use this notion to justify a "moral" condemnation of homosexuality, since this process works with many gay couples in practice. To make it work, both partners need to enter their pairing with a certain pre-existing **balance**, and a desire to find daily good living in their relationship instead of a highly individualized expression of idealistic values. Narcissistic love seems on the one hand individualistic in that it seems to give the person absolute control over his erotic choices (at the fantasy level, at least), and yet at the same time collectivistic, in that is seems to relate to a collectively defined aesthetic idea. Indeed, "realism" in family relationships is held by some as an inevitable step in individual growth. (Oh, how those grade schools marked "progress of the pupil as an individual" and "progress of the individual as a member of the group.")

Narcissism, after all, has its selling points. It reminds one of the mediocrity of much of the human scene, of how conventional life often deteriorates into false submission—even timidity—and recklessness, and of how it tolerates premature degradation of individuals. Indeed, today narcissism is a good motivator for physical fitness, good health habits, and the avoidance of tobacco, excessive alcohol, and recreational drugs. *It takes a narcissist to appreciate the full potential of another person if (and only if) that potential partner's gifts really are extraordinary.* But at some point, one needs to look beyond one's own bellybutton.

Furthermore, discussion of affiliation, narcissism and balance in relationships depends on just what one means by "relationship." If being "married" is one's expected goal, the imbalance of a pairing seems a much bigger issue than it is for someone who allows himself or herself to have many "significant others" without full sexual relations.

None of this is said with the intent to moralize. We just want to describe what really happens in uncontrolled experiments. But narcissism and affiliation bear a definite relation to moral thinking. Moral systems that emphasize collective welfare, egalitarianism, or security may emphatically reject narcissistic and affiliative processes, particularly for objects chosen by individuals. Conservative morality, with an emphasis on simple moral "truths" easily seen in the Bible (as fundamentalists read it), emphasizes anchoring the individual's sexual psyche in conventional gender obligations and monogamous marriage, to the extent that individuals see affiliation as just a temptation. Fidelity to these obligations is supposed to ensure a fair amount of justice, and homosexuality becomes an unacceptable distraction.

Liberal morality (sometimes appearing to be based on situational thinking or on rejection of simple readings of the Bible) becomes focused on egalitarianism and accepts homosexuality as long as it follows, in its own way (gay marriage), the "everybody's beautiful" myth. Objectivism accepts certain imbalance in opportunity and wealth and puts all the responsibility for the choice and process of affiliation back up on the person, as long as the person is totally responsible for himself and realizes he needs a bit of charity to grow as a real sovereign individual. Narcissism, taken as a whole, is frowned upon in general because, if carried out by most people, it would tend to make society more "Darwinian" and leave average people (assuming the culture no longer lets them "hide" behind marriage) with no one who will care about them.

The public perception that homosexuality (particularly among young men) is fundamentally narcissistic undermines sincere attempts by gays to gain legal recognition for committed relationships, for the right to adopt and parent, and even to serve in the military. On the other hand, love and power generate more than a zero-sum game: If you care about someone you choose by your own standards (however narcissisticly) it becomes easier to care about others who do not immediately appeal. Even so, if someone has never learned to care about others with narcissism, he will become a suspect "single" viewed as a bit creepy (as in a passage in Joe Babcock's Salinger-like novel *The Tragedy of Miss Geneva Flowers*,[78] where the first person teenage narrator speculates on what it would be like to be 40 and still enjoys only his ephebophilia.)

Are "unbalanced personalities" more likely to be narcissistic? Perhaps they would see a narcissistic object choice as more expressive of individuality. On the other hand, a balanced personality might find more individual satisfaction in procreation (propagating his own biological substance and proudly accepting as a parent what one bears from his genetic lottery) and might see "hero worship" as a kind of collectivism!

One can look at narcissism as a catalyst for a chemical reaction, as explained in those hated high school chemistry courses. It is helpful in stimulating creative expression in relationships but it does not constitute creativity in itself. The creative challenge is in finding something special to love or to value in a partner, and to perform as the one person that can both recognize and develop those special gifts. It is not sufficient just to care about another person when that person can make one feel turned on. We need to keep our social preoccupation with "looks" (whether in a gay male context or not) in the proper perspective.

8:

THE INFORMATION TECHNOLOGY JOB MARKET: WHAT HAS HAPPENED AND WHAT WILL HAPPEN

Everybody rejoiced when a nerdy teenager Peter Parker, played by a gentle Tobey Maguire, blossoms quite visibly into manhood with great power and great responsibility, like a male Cinderella in the recent Marvel Comics-based movie *Spider Man*. When I was growing up in the 40s, 50s, and early 60s, I successfully fought for the notion that an awkward and physically backward boy could legitimize himself by succeeding academically. I rather got away with it but judging from the controversy over bullying in many of our public school systems, many teens do not. Yet, a new icon has appeared: a lonely but winsome teen who stays home and pounds away on his computer, developing his own kind of competitiveness with a technical and often mainly mechanical, basically masculine, curiosity.

The results from this trend vary. Some teens fear and resent authority or the notion of conventional competitiveness, so they distinguish themselves by writing and propagating viruses and worms or by hacking into classified websites (sometimes this requires real mental gymnastics to deal with buffer overflows, packets and bit-streams). At the other extreme, some start real businesses and become millionaires. These enterprises range from firewall companies to legitimate music review services. Not all were physical sissies like me. Sean Fanning, who taught himself peer-to-peer computing and started Napster (and I leave aside the legal controversy over music copyrights for the moment) might have been a baseball player.

Nevertheless we have a new stereotype to ponder, the "geek." Not that this is negative, pejorative, dilettante or anti-social at all. Navy officer Paul Thomasson, who challenged the military gay ban while stationed at the Pentagon, had characterized himself as an all-purpose "geekolator." A tech company in Minneapolis, The Geek Squad, boasts that its employees would rather play with computers (hardware as much as programming) on Saturday nights than go on dates. My financial planner tells me that his personal computer desktop was set up by his I.T. guy. There is something reassuring about working with technology, with things, and particularly with abstractions. For one thing, you don't have to peddle to other people.

Geek culture, however, is still relatively new to the information technology world, even if that culture is distorting it. It is useful to go back into history and look at the culture of information technology as a "profession" and to understand how it evolved. I can weigh in on this with thirty-five years worth of personal experience.

Perhaps the ultimate personal encounter with this kind of geek mentality occurred in the summer of 2002 when a woman at a telemarketing (or "telefunding") job (that is how "low"—like the Nasdaq—I have gone, although I am raising funds for a non-profit and good cause) asked me if I could fix the time-of-day counter on her cell phone. Without directions ("documentation"), I could not. The phone was very different from mine. "But a systems analyst does computers," she protested. "Systems analysts figure out how computers work and fix them." And a cell phone is effectively a computer, a PDA perhaps, even if it's wireless. This reminded me of an occasion twenty years before when a woman at work asked if I could change her flat tire because a man was (in her mind) supposed to do such things for a woman. (I also hear people say, about phone bank jobs, that they are the only kind of jobs some people can get—but they can raise money for good causes and sometimes the commissions can provide a reasonable income in tough times.)

The idea of computers as the basis of a new profession probably goes back to World War II, when British and American intelligence developed enormous machines to break Nazi codes (as in the movie *Enigma*). Government and business quickly recognized the potential economic value of large-scale computing in defense, space, and later commerce, and the engineering work for it grew quickly after World War II, as did programming languages. By the 1950s, businesses often had crude computer systems, sometimes EAM equipment with plug boards, to do accounting and inventory. Schools used such equipment for class schedules and grades. IBM, Burroughs, Univac, NCR, Control Data and RCA (and especially Cray) all worked on larger computers, which at first were divided into "scientific" and "business" categories.

By the mid 1960s the "general purpose" IBM 360 series had evolved and would be answered by other vendors. Scientific computing, such as mission command and control, was really quite well developed in the 1960s. Higher languages like FORTRAN and COBOL came into considerable use, and jobs for programmers at both the machine and conceptual level developed. Even COBOL, an English-like language designed for business use, has its origins with the work of Dr. Grace Hopper working for the Naval Reserve.

I dove into this with summer jobs with the Navy in the 1960s. The academic background for computer programmers then was usually mathematics or electrical engineering. "Computer science" as an academic discipline and major came into being in the late 1960s, just a bit too late for me.

The winding down of Vietnam and defense cuts followed by the oil and Mid East crises produced a recession in the 1972-1974 period (and actually a mini dip around 1970) but the computer field continued to grow. Major commercial employers, especially banks and insurance companies as well as manufacturers, invested heavily into bread-and-butter mainframe batch and online applications in the 1970s and early 1980s, especially in areas like accounting, inventory, investment, as well as health care and welfare programs usually developed by government contractors. In the earliest days defense culture heavily influenced information technology values, and some companies like EDS frankly and openly preferred to hire ex-military people. Many companies enforced strict dress codes in order to maintain a public image of professionalism.

This culture would gradually change as civilian commercial applications became more important. The growing commercialism would help IBM edge out all of its competitors in the mainframe business. By the late 1970s, having an IBM background clearly gave an advantage in the job market. Soon CICS (the major IBM teleprocessing monitor) and various databases would become important components in one's background. People would change jobs to "get IBM" and again to get the expected hands-on experience coding CICS and various databases (especially IMS and then DB2).

Since early programming jobs tended to emphasize meticulous, almost "feminine" attention to detail and mental concentration, the field of systems analysis—the translation of business requirements (and, often enough, specification and assembly of business requirements) into detailed procedural instructions (such as "structured English" and even pseudocode) for programmers became an informal discipline of its own. The job of systems analyst was a natural promotion for a programmer, with higher level business responsibilities and less focus on "the trees." Gradually, the concept of a *full systems life cycle* was nurtured.

Another important development in the 1970s especially was programmer productivity. In the earliest days of keypunched cards there was considerable emphasis on desk-checking and tedious, methodical dump analysis, since programmers often had only one "shot" a day or had to use scheduled time at night. Without the ability to solve problems without excessive machine use, one could not keep a job. But in the 1970s employee terminals became more common, first at vendors (like Univac) other than IBM. Some companies would have a "tube city" room but by the 1980s most employees had their own dedicated mainframe terminals. Productivity dump-analysis and debugging tools developed and relieved the need for tedium.

A further enhancement of mainframe culture in most commercial shops would be the development of separation of functions and security access, by the late 1980s. Generally, programmers would no longer be able to update production data without specific access.

All of this gradual improvement in information technology tended to lead to a new generalist job category, the "programmer-analyst." The responsibilities for combining technical business requirements analysis with coding, testing, implementation and support could become one position. This led to more cost-savings for employers and often benefited the associate as well. A computer professional could earn a steady high income without formal movement into or deliberate grooming for management (often distasteful for the somewhat introverted character of many information technology people during those days).

Even so he could become more valuable to his organization while being himself. Often he or she became the guru of some company-specific application in regular production and would be paid very well to stay (sometimes at the risk of not keeping up with technical skills likely to be expected by other employers). Companies could get into positions of severe exposure if such key people left.

On the other hand, the computer professional was held to a very high standard of accuracy and dependability for his system, which would repeatedly process huge volumes of data in production, often 24 x 7, so the idea of being on "nightcall" (and performing reliably when on such detail—there is no "they"!) grew rapidly. With no union to represent them and no clear direction from certification bodies as to proper human resources policies, salaried programmers were often expected to put in uncompensated overtime. Availability for night support became perceived as a "moral issue" in some shops.

There were, of course, many other kinds of jobs. For example, data centers would be populated by operators who were paid hourly for shifts that ran at all times. Mainframe technical support tended to become a different kind of job, salaried but much more likely to be done off-hours. Technical support professionals (and so-called "systems programmers") did not write their own programs; rather, they installed system software provided by major vendors and then maintained the software by installing and testing patches and fixes.

The job market diversified in other areas. Consulting companies hired programmers to staff large projects at customer companies. Typical assignments ran from a few months to several years but sometimes programmers were compensated even when "on the bench," a good time for training. Vendors would develop "asset persons," firefighters who drove from one customer site to another.

In the late 1980s and early 1990s a major sea change began to develop in the market. Mergers (including hostile takeovers) and leveraged buyouts led to major data center consolidations including application consolidations and then layoffs. Gradually less capable programmers would be weeded out of the market. However, new opportunities that gradually changed the whole culture of computing emerged.

In the mainframe area companies tended to migrate from homemade or "in house" systems to purchased packages from large software vendors. Actually, packages (like CFO from IBM in the life insurance industry), often written in assembler, had been in use for years and offered quite sophisticated end- user options. Even so shops had always spent a lot of time and money on in-house interfaces and add-ons. Newer packages, like Vantage in the life insurance business and various financial packages like

MSA from Dun and Bradstreet, tended to try to "rule the world" and force customers into mastering whole new systems cultures.

These vendor packages began to affect the mainframe job market, as employers needed people with detailed expertise in these packages. Sometimes these packages would tend to drive applications programmers into technical support areas and potentially compromise the separation of functions concept that businesses had developed as part of their "best practices" for security and audit.

More important were the development first of the personal computer before 1980 (remember the Commodore and the Osborne, as well as TRS-80?) and then the opening of Internet, which (though originally conceived as a defense and academic facility) was turned loose to the public by the National Science Foundation in 1992 toward the end of the "first Bush administration." Even before the Internet became public, the personal computer was seen as providing opportunities for scalable and cheaper applications such as retail point-of-sale.

The late 1980s saw the rapid increase in practical individual computing, with word-processing packages and then database management packages (when DBase III+ had its heyday). Smaller companies (such as a public policy think tank that I worked for) faced the choice between renting mainframe disk space and computer time, and bringing applications in-house onto personal computers that they could "control." For a time, mainframe platforms like IBM VM tried to mimic PC-style modes of operation.

At the same time, companies tried to provide mainframe-style database technologies for the PC, such as when Rbase (Microrim) and then DBase IV (then, Ashton-Tate) offered relational SQL processing. The mini-computer market (such as the VAX, Silverlake/AS400, MAI Basic 4) had grown steadily into the mid 1990s, and emphasized less verbose "PC type" languages such as C and Basic, and the Unix (as opposed to the IBM mainframe DOS and MVS) operating system. Larger telecommunications companies (building on earlier defense-oriented experience) had already learned how to work with the operating systems and languages to build their own commercial networks when the Internet became available.

The rules of the game changed quickly as the Internet developed. Some of the changes were applicable to the mainframe world. For example, database technology gradually pulled away from specific design models (IMS and Focus for hierarchal, IDMS and Adabas for network paradigm) to relational models: first DB2 for IBM, and then Sybase and Oracle on Unix-style (or Microsoft) networks. Object-oriented computing ("responsibility driven design") began to compete with procedural programming ("structured design").

During the 1990s the mainframe job market remained strong because of the attention paid to the Y2K problem. All along, there was developing a new emphasis on formatting interfaces for the end user, especially the external consumer, who would use the Internet to make purchases. This worldview required a new emphasis on scalability and portability of applications. So-called "sexy" languages like C, C++ and java (and now C#, in connection with Microsoft's .NET), as well as visually-driven development packages like Powerbuilder and (most of all) Visual Basic, were much more adaptable to this scalability requirement than was mainframe-style programming in COBOL and early 90s releases of CICS. (COBOL, however, does now have a rich object-oriented facility.) Unix, Windows and MacIntosh operating systems were all considered more flexible than the stodgy mainframe MVS with its verbose batch JCL.

After the Y2K event was traversed with (to some hungry minds) relatively few problems, the demand for mainframe skills seemed to fall off of a cliff. This seemed particularly true during the economic slowdown towards the end of 2000, well before the 9-11 tragedy. On the surface, this seems to happen because client-server architecture is much more flexible for the new economy. But there are questions. Scalability and portability have to be weighed against the need, in the short term, for a large number of software licenses and people to support the various components.

In some conservative environments, mainframe could still be economical. IBM has developed an embedded Unix System Facility within mainframe OS390 and is in a position to offer very disciplined management of all client-server production environments with mainframe-style source and implementation control, along with large database server capacity. The open architecture of modern computing has, of course, made it very vulnerable to virus, worm and packet-sniffing attacks—a development that leads to a tremendous demand for geeks with in-depth security skills, perhaps in a pace that exceeds the ability of companies to do background checks. But even mainframe environments had their vulnerabilities, as when source and load module control was not carefully enforced.

All of this does relate to a cultural divide between older "baby boomer" professionals (like myself) and younger geeks. Okay, I over-simplify with these loaded words, but I did find the transition to client-server, at least in a support role, difficult. The knowledge base in a practical corporate environment tended to be fragmented, with different components in varied languages patched together with various kinds of complicated interfaces. There was an unexpected emphasis on being able to solve problems that the programmer had never seen before, with business applications written in cryptic languages or poorly documented implementations done by consultants who were long since gone. The younger temperament vouches for quick learning curves and quick development, with source and scripting languages that seem more mechanical and less verbose than structured COBOL, command level CICS, and various mainframe 4GL's. Computer magazines have sometimes predicted that older mainframe or procedural programmers won't be able to grasp the mental connections (implementations through interfaces) required by object-oriented design.

Younger programmers tend to learn the newer languages on campuses as an engineering discipline. A major factor in the technical culture is that the aim of computing is changing, not only with the new emphasis on the external consumer but also with the interest in passing data in "peer-to-peer" fashion among customers or stakeholders without always monitoring all transactions from one database. The low-level C or assembler coding of "firmware," for those devices that "Q" so proudly displayed in James Bond movies, seems to have increased relative to the market, making the emphasis on engineering more prominent.

Yet vendors are promising a very disciplined, almost mainframe-style environment for future enterprises. Sun proposes to handle almost any conceivable corporate computing problem with complete implementation of its java platforms, with a new emphasis on XML data, schemas and style sheets to manipulate the content sent to the end user. Java (and now Microsoft's C#) can do practically anything, including managing threads and system performance, so there is a tendency for the intellectual disciplines for business logic and underlying system software support to merge into one seamless whole.

Once again, the distinction between business logic and systems maintenance can become blurred (a *big* security concern) but Enterprise Java Beans are offered as a new way to implement such a separation. The "java final solution" carries portability to its ultimate incarnation. On the other hand, Microsoft (having displaced IBM as the ruler of the world and inviting plenty of litigation in the process) offers .NET, with the ability to handle almost any language, as the ultimate solution for parsing information sent to the end user.

Part of understanding the future job market harkens for a review of just what we use our information for. I took advantage of the technology boom of the mid-1990s to self-publish a huge book at low cost. But others saw technology as a cheap way to mass-market simple products and services (the opposite of developing the rich content of books and movies). Part of the problem with the "Startup.com" phenomenon and subsequent pre-9-11 bust was the superficiality of what was being offered to an impatient consumer.

There is a lot of emphasis, especially with .NET, in point-to-point messaging capability, as if one's top priority were knowing the just-in-time inventory levels of a supplier five minutes ago, or of reliable wireless and mobile email communications when setting up a clandestine luncheon rendez-vous (for me, at least, in Boston's Legal Seafoods). Yet IBM, Sun and Microsoft all propose flexible visions of computing that can support rich and educational multimedia content development as well as major business infrastructure upgrade. The most glaring example of which might be the need for a new air traffic control system and for new systems in intelligence and law enforcement to connect the dots.

Where does this leave the job seeker, particularly the experienced professional, in today's market? Between a rock and a hard place? Maybe, because the market is sputtering in so many directions as it tries to get started again. Already there is demand for mainframe programmers but generally for very narrowly defined skill-sets for relatively short term W-2 contracts. There has been some controversy in the literature (as with the Meta Group) as to whether companies will soon need older mainframe programmers as the college campuses fail to replace those that leave and retire. In April, 2002 Bob Weinstein published a "Tech Watch" syndicated column in which he predicted that companies would seen have to search for large number of mainframe programmers in their 50s and 60s to maintain their backbone legacy systems.[79] Whether outsourcing these systems off-shore will eliminate this need remains to be seen, especially in light of world instability. Outsourcers may not have the business knowledge and communications skills to maintain intricate legacy systems as they run in production, so some demand of older professionals who grew up in the business could continue.[80]

Sometimes there may appear sudden interest from employers in specific areas, as in the summer of 2002 when carriers for Medicaid programs and other health care providers suddenly began recruiting (at least for short term contracts) mainframe people to comply with the Health Insurance Portability and Accountability Act.[81] At the same time, the overwhelming majority of open positions on jobs web sites seem to be with newer "open systems" technologies.

With a profession changing gears so suddenly and unpredictably, one of the most critical issues seems to be how it should define its notion of "professionalism." Information technology has historically been one of the least "regulated" fields for professionals. Medicine, law, financial planning, accounting, actuarial and engineering all have processes of certification and regulation (shared by industry certification processes and state regulation) that are far more controlled. The growing popularity of advanced degrees in information technology may prove useful in providing some organized basis for disciplined knowledge, as is the case with MBA's. Even graduate students in I.T. seem little informed about the heavily controlled processes in mainframe shops.

There have been various attempts to bring certification to the information business. The Institute for the Certification of Computer Professionals offers general certification that is based mostly on passing conceptual exams in areas such as business systems, systems design, software engineering and security; the offering in specific languages is somewhat limited but growing. A company called Brainbench offers adaptive online testing and certification in many very specific programming languages and disciplines. Software vendors have for a few years offered their own performance-graded "boot camps" and certifications, mostly in newer technologies.

Many of these appear to be directed at younger workers, often those without college degrees—again, going along with the idea of information technology as a "trade" as well as a "profession." Some computer stores actually employ high-school students as desktop repair technicians and enable the students to earn A+ certifications before graduating from high school!

At the same time, in a market where supply of candidates presently exceeds demand, employers have demanded very specific, job-ready skills from applicants. Their demands require particular combinations of specific skills with recent experience, often with considerable practical depth and hands-on practice beyond a certification or campus course. To some candidates the behavior of employers and recruiters probably seems erratic. But as the economy gradually stabilizes into a slow-growth pattern, employers will probably be more concerned with candidate goals and with some kind of direction and consistency in their past careers.

All of this brings up the testy problem of career motivation. I.T. people have, for the price of eternal vigilance regarding the production business systems that they support (often including regular batch cycles), long enjoyed the relative comfort of steady job demand growth without too much hucksterism. The trend towards client-server requires the professional to be much quicker to pick up new non-linear skills, even at his own time and expense, whereas the large mainframe applications of the past often used relatively small parts of a professional's potential knowledge base.

I.T. people have often disdained being too closely identified publicly with the business customers or interests that they serve (and some I.T. professionals have a particular disdain for people like telemarketers, multi-level marketing intermediaries or the car salesman from *Fargo*, whom they see as parasites unable to hold down "real jobs" or as earning a living with a paradigm predicated on bothering people with unsolicited calls or spam, although I.T. people may be surprised by the regimentation and the hard work in projecting "belief" that goes with some marketing positions[82]). There is an ethical tradeoff here. We can envision a paradigm where large businesses are more willing to develop associates' careers in exchange for a public loyalty to the aims of the business (and a willingness to invest heavily in business as well as technical expertise). Professionals who are uncomfortable with a commitment to one kind of business (especially to the point of moving into management and advocating the company publicly) would be expected to emphasize technical curiosity for its own sake. A few years ago where a particularly geeky coworker chided me for my "astonishing lack of curiosity" about all the little technical niches on my desktop—he saw mechanical curiosity as the justification for his position and an excuse to remain apolitical about everything!

This paradigm means that I.T. professionals would regularly take certification tests in a variety of areas to make sure that they are committed to keeping up with less-frequently used skills (like unaided dump analysis, for that matter, on the mainframe). The explosive growth in software, along with the change in design paradigms, means that today I.T. professionals will have to remain very deliberate and diligent in keeping themselves trained with specific expertise, regardless of the immediate demands in jobs that they have now. "Resume stuffing" with lists of areas in which one has light or superficial experience would be discouraged, and professionals would have to weigh carefully the balance between versatility and commitment with specific expertise to skills that may not always remain in high demand. Employers should make keeping up with technology a major performance evaluation component and requirement. Geek curiosity, while inviting the acceleration of machine intelligence, presents a certain paradox with regard to professionalism, as it is predicated upon readiness to solve new problems created by others, and develop real expertise very quickly as a way of belonging in a profession. Is "geek professionalism" an oxymoron? Perhaps not if it is defined by its own mechanical inquisitiveness.

Computer User has provided some sobering accounts of how demand is changing. Jim Thompson in "Hot Careers in a Cool Market"[83] wrote that skills having to do with infrastructure, administration, peer-to-peer contacts, security (of course) and even multimedia were in much more demand than "content related" application programming skills. Robert McGarvey predicts that more jobs will migrate to the administration area in his discussion of certification.[84] At least one company, Advanced Internet Technologies in Fayetteville, N.C. has tried to model itself after the military,[85] as had (to an extent, especially with its prudish dress codes) Electronic Data Systems (EDS) back in the 1960s and 1970s.

The Information Technology Association of America presented (in May 2002) a report, "Bouncing Back: Jobs, Skills, and the Continuing Demand for IT Workers," discussed the paradox of overall reduced reductions in positions together with unfilled positions in specialized areas. The shakeout in the I.T. job market may indeed force most computer professionals to focus and narrow their goals. No longer will it be reasonable to sit in a comfortable place and (even given dedication to systems one has personally developed or worked on) and collect a good paycheck without a strategy for advancement and for addressing the needs of specific kinds of customers. Technical people will have to focus on the details of their craft and accept opportunity costs (going "Greyhound" and leaving controversies outside of their expertise areas to others) until they are prepared to move into focused business areas for which they feel comfortable with a public commitment.

Ten years ago in the previous recession, there was a certain disdain for middle management, as companies flattened their organizations with wider spans of control. The conventional wisdom was to market a job-ready, hands-on capability in a practical way, and some people thought that managers should prove that they could do the jobs of their reports. I have encountered the "Peter Principle" idea that managers or even business analysts weren't "smart" enough to remain "real programmers," just as I have encountered the opposing view that some programmers just don't want to "grow up" and advance! That technical focus is still valid (as many positions seem to look for exact skill matches), but today there seems to be more emphasis to multi-task with the ability to assume leadership roles and formal or project management roles (with soft skills) when needed.

Whatever an I.T. professional's choice, Internet culture will force him or her to become public about his or her professional goals and business associations, and even in a recessionary environment some companies prefer to hire only professionals prepared for a long-term somewhat publicly visible commitment rather than short term W2 contractors (receivng no benefits except regular social security tax rates and liability insurance). There is a distinction between **contractor** and **consultant**. Like it or not, you will become what you do.

I spent thirty-one years in I.T. after leaving the Army and went thirty years without a layoff, with very dependable income. But one Thursday morning in December 2001 a Novell server told me that my account was disabled. Ten minutes later a director was offering a handshake as he awarded a long severance package. I had remained a freelancer since that moment. As of September 2002, I have yet to log on to a work computer.

9:

SELF-PUBLISHING: ETHICAL AND LEGAL TRENDS

The self-publication of my *Do Ask, Do Tell* and subsequent books or monographs, maintaining the associated websites, and developing possible film treatment proposals have all provided quite an adventure and odyssey for me. Yes, as I got into my fifties, I saw writing as a likely second career for me and I recognized that technology could provide opportunities not practical in earlier generations. In time, I began to recognize a plethora of potential legal and ethical issues as I developed my writings but continued to work in a salaried job at the same time. I have provided some textbook-style treatment of these problems on my web site (hppub.com) but for this book sequel I want to cover the material with a chronological personal account.

It is true that I have self-published on political and social matters in which I am not a "recognized" authority in the customary sense of academic degrees and "professional" career. But on such issues as the military (the draft and the "don't ask don't tell" policy) and "family values" I am certainly a practical expert on the subtle and complicated ways that they affect gays and lesbians. I found it more productive to publish my own insights on these problems rather than just send money to political action groups and follow their marching orders.

But the process of challenging the military ban opened a pandora's box that progressively examined the processes of public commercial speech on controversial areas. I gambled that my editorial content, published and displayed passively on the Internet and e-commerce sites, would sell itself and sell me, without my having had to develop credentials by competing adversarily in some narrow public policy area. At the same time, I eschewed publicly visible "advancement" in corporate information technology, feeling that pursuing it would misrepresent who I am. I could not hide behind pseudonyms; I wanted my public reputation connected to my ideas.

I first "got published" in 1974 by a tiny gay newspaper in New Brunswick, New Jersey (*The Gay Old Times*). In 1977 I typewrote an essay on freedom and responsibility that would get published by the Arizona newage group *Understanding* in 1978.

During the 1980s I sometimes got newspaper letters published or read on television stations regarding the way the gay press tried to represent gay "victims" of AIDS. I created some controversy in Dallas by trying, on my own, to establish a bridge with religious groups on the AIDS issues.

When President Clinton (even before his election) resurrected the military gay ban as a political issue in 1992 and 1993 (actually the issue had been bootstrapped by Keith Meinhold's television interview in May 1992 and then Joe Steffan's sensational book, *Honor Bound*), I awoke from a certain psychological stagnation. The arguments in use resonated with what had happened to me in college during those Cold War days. I wrote a series of four letters to the conservative *Washington Times* and all of these miniatures were published.

In the early days of debate, I saw the ban in (conservative) terms of personal privacy violation and exclusion, and I honestly believed and argued that some form of moderate "don't ask don't tell" was the only acceptable resolution. I was able to access someone with ties to the White House in a series of meetings, along with research (such as my own submarine visit) that led to a series of various letters to Congress and the White House. All this time, my public exposure was relatively limited. Yet, I sought opportunities to publish in various other gay and mainstream periodicals.

In 1994, I started getting published in the newsletter, *The Quill*, for Gays and Lesbians for Individual Liberty. In 1995, I took over as editor (for four years). I also appeared frequently in the Colorado Springs *Ground Zero News* (an ironic title now) as it published my "White House Letter," and *Forward Observer* (for gay veterans). None of these opportunities paid. Given the parade of public-issue oriented books in the early and mid-1990s, I began to feel that I could offer a unique perspective if I wrote a large book of my own. By late summer of 1994, when it was becoming clear that the "don't ask don't tell" policy would fail in practice, I had decided to write a book to be called *Do Ask Do Tell*. By the time I had moved into a larger apartment in August 1995, I was working steadily on it but went through three other organizations of my material until I settled on the autobiographical but topical six-chapter form, "like a symphony."

I contacted a literary agent in New York. He provided a critical reading of the project. At first, his reaction was quite promising, but then other military people who had fought the ban were starting to encounter resistance at publishers, as there were already several books on the ban in the market (competing, as they said in rejection letters, for "coffee table space"). But my book would be broader, to provide a broader argument for gay rights as a subset of individual rights.

I was motivated by the inadequacy of the way gay issues were usually argued publicly, presenting gays as a victim class and tending to appeal to the lowest common denominator for short term political gains. In time, I began to explore the self-publishing options. I found that I could negotiate very good prices for proofreading, typesetting, and printing (book manufacturing) from persons or vendors (that normally offer extremely varied prices, especially with printing) who seemed to believe that a project like this ought to be done.

Self-publishing, even by the mid 1990s, was a much more reasonable option financially than **subsidy** publishing, where the author pays a publishing company to take full responsibility for manufacturing and distributing the book (or a variation, **vanity** publishing for limited distribution within a particular community). Formally, the only legal step that I needed was to form a proprietorship, register the assumed name with local government (then, Fairfax County, Virginia), including particularly getting a sales tax license, and obtain an ISBN publisher's number and series of book suffixes from R.R. Bowker, the ISBN Agency. I officially took possession of my first printing and mailed the required copies to the Library of Congress on July 11, 1997. This event, making the book available to anyone prepared to pay a fair market price for a legal copy, amounts to formal publication.

During this period, I had been working as a computer programmer for a company in the Washington metro area that specialized in selling life insurance to military officers as one of its major and identifying lines of business. Common sense might suggest that this situation could present a conflict of interest. If my writings and books attracted publicity, they could provide embarrassment for the "fraternal" employer, and to depending upon a customer set with which one feels compelled to criticize publicly seems like a breach of ethics. Furthermore, the potential availability to me of data from this targeted customer set, even though not actually used (and in fact it never was), might create the appearance of a violation of the privacy of these customers.

However, in early 1995 the company was bought by a larger company in Minneapolis, and this merger could dilute the importance of the military customer base or provide job opportunities (after the merger) without loss of seniority and without involvement with the military customer base. I discussed this matter with an attorney associated with the ban (Paul Thomasson's attorney) in May 1996 and then informed the company. There followed some due diligence meetings with human resources and memos, and I arranged a transfer to Minneapolis to take place in

September 1997. I drove out and moved Labor Day weekend, quite a memorable journey now. In suburban Chicago, a cop stopped me for speeding but let me go when he saw the book on the back seat!

Shortly after arriving in Minneapolis I became active with the Libertarian Party of Minnesota. A graduating senior from Hamline University (joking, "Public speaking is easy") arranged for me to speak at his school. The speech would be broadcast several times on a local cable station. Later I would speak at the University of Minnesota and at a local Unitarian group.

The initial PQN (print quantity needed) printing was about 350 (small because of the size of the book, about 180,000 words) and I was able to sell it out by the fall of 1999. Maybe about 60 copies were given away but the others were actually sold. I found a distributor in Minneapolis, the Bookmen (recently purchased by Ingram), who was willing to buy about 30 of them and they were all sold. A major gay bookstore chain bought 15 and most of these were sold. I submitted the books to Amazon.com and Barnes and Noble, and sometimes got email orders directly.

Admittedly there were some technical issues with the book. A reading of the *Chicago Manual of Style* (from the University of Chicago Press) shows that commercial book publishing requires some scale to achieve a high standard of manufacturing quality, including typesetting, copyediting and removing all possible errors as well as consistency to intricate style rules. Information technology has greatly reduced these costs for large publishers, who feel considerable bottom line pressure (from Wall Street) to cut costs. As a result, there has been a tendency for more errors and typos to creep even into books from large trade publishers.

I was of course far from immune from this, and one problem that I had in early 1997 as I prepared the document for submission was considerable last minute changes by me to the content, as such topics as gay marriage, the military ban and the Communications Decency Act constantly generated more news. So there are more typos (most of them microscopic, like leaving off the "d" in "and") than I would feel proud of. One particular gaff that got missed was stating that the Bill of Rights is 160 years old; the correct number was 210! On many copies, after I received them, I pasted a plastic overlay with the number '210' onto the back cover.

By 2000, I was still receiving orders. For a second edition I turned to the new concept of on-demand printing, and an e-publishing company to keep the book in print economically. Of course, this gave me another chance to fix the typos. I was working with an example of what the industry calls a **cooperative publisher**. I had also self-published a brief supplement, *Our Fundamental Rights*, at the end of 1998. On-demand printing systems reduce inventory and can provide an effective vehicle for new authors to introduce their ideas to the market and make themselves known, although it is often difficult to attain high sales volumes or sales ranks on e-commerce sites with on-demand alone. Some self-published books, especially those that target very specific audiences or particularly regional subject matter, do well in print runs but they should always be printed by **book manufacturers** rather than other kinds of printers. Recently, some universities have been offering their best Ph. D. dissertations for sale in commercial bookseller markets, and this situation could be described as academic cooperative publishing.

During these two or three years, I would attend other discussions about self-publishing. Self-published and cooperatively published books range in content, from fiction (especially gay fiction), to self-help or inspirational books, to cookbooks and how-to books. Some self-publishers arrange a pool of investors on their own, and these may be family members or relatives (and some promoters of self-publishing encouraging hitting up relatives for gung-ho support). Most quit their day jobs and expect the sales volume to provide enough for them to live on, but I did not. Some "self-published" books really are more representative of corporate publishing, as when a restaurant publishes a cookbook of its favorite recipes. Insurance and financial service companies often assemble self-help materials that would be very sellable in the commercial book world but choose to distribute these books only through agents.

I have heard the opinion that "self-publishing doesn't count." Book reviewers sometimes report seeing self-published personal memoirs that were better left circulated among families or private communities but not original enough to interest the general public, and sometimes of poor production quality. A few self-published books, when marketed well, have become best sellers, and a number of literary authors (like Walt Whitman) were largely self-published. Self-publishing, after all, is all about creating one's own product and selling it—the fundamental "theorem" of capitalism, perhaps, a process that ought to be accepted in a economy that now needs some more original "real wealth" if it is to start performing again.

To some extent, one wonders if assembling a pool of investors counts as self-publishing, but it does so in that (following practices better known in independent film) there are disclosure rules and various legally expected practices having to do with the involvement of investors in actual production of the intellectual property. The subtle point is, perhaps, that if one really can tap into OPM (other people's money), that resource increases the author's credibility, just as being published by an outside third party (a genuine trade publisher) and investing nothing of one's own funds adds credibility. Of course, public financial success is another way to establish accountability.

Of course, I did the opposite. Since my costs were very low and I was still working, I did not need immediate results from my little business. In Minneapolis, I would rent a secure high-rise apartment two blocks from work to save commuting costs and, particularly, time.

A friend that I had met in the workplace was running an ISP with shared collocated rack space at a collocation provider in Maryland, so I signed up with him with a very inexpensive and, as it turned out, reliable web hosting service. My original purpose was to update the book contents with running footnote files. Quickly, I found that I could attract readers by posting the entire book content on the site for convenient browsing. Soon the search engines found and indexed my materials. This turned out to be a very efficient form of passive advertising (without telemarketing, mailing lists or spam). Some persons did order the book directly after finding it this way. More often, book buyers for public libraries would order the book from various sections of the country.

At this point, we come to the issue of ethics in reverse. Most problems in the press regarding conflict of interest deal with accountants or financial advisors who are given incentives to be less than objective in their professional services. Here, the problems center around the rather obscure intellectual property law concept of "right of publicity," an idea very sensitive in the entertainment world but rather ignored elsewhere. If I write material that I consider important, then I have to consider how I use may name in public in other work. In self-publishing, debate abstraction can become problematical, as readers who know the author will instantiate specific allegations anyway. The hallmark of typical adversarial debate is that if you bring up a counter-argument even as a supposition it invites a specific peril.

The first clue of problems came in 1998 when Congress proposed and then actually passed the Child Online Protection Act. More details are available in another essay in this booklet. I signed up with Electronic Frontier Foundation as a plaintiff. The overall paradigm that would soon affect my thinking in other areas was that, to promote myself, I was taking undue advantage of new technology in an unsupervised fashion to draw attention to myself and, particularly, place adult and controversial materials (though not pornographic) within the reach of children or, as arguments would develop, within the reach of customers or stakeholders or other persons or entities (like employers) associated with me. On the other hand, the Internet, for most entrepreneurs, suggested a "numbers game" paradigm. Micro unit-costed unsolicited mass marketing to enough prospects will generate enough business to make money.

Of course, I could fine-tune my motive easily. Conventional political debate tends to be adversarial with various political pressure groups (however well-meaning) soliciting funds from the public (and asking for form letters to lawmakers) to present their often oversimplified views about issues such as gay rights, minorities, discrimination or hate crimes. Intellectual honesty does not come from such a process, however tied it may be to how most people perceive a representative democracy's functions.

For example, one can envision a political compromise that embraces ENDA and hate crimes legislation for gays but that denies gays in the military, gay marriage and gay adoptions. Such a compromise skirts the difficult moral question of gays "carrying their weight" in a cultural system. But for an individual writer to get into this skirts danger.

In time, other potential problems would surface. In early 1999 there occurred at least one arrest where a software professional had used his own website to manipulate the stock price of his employer. Later in 1999, there were reports of incidents where hospital or child welfare employees were fired for off-duty participation in pornographic websites that were potentially available to the employer's stakeholders. Also, there were incidents where individuals anonymously posted derogatory comments from home about their employers on investor trash boards (as on Yahoo!), and were fired when their employers were able to subpoena their names from these ISP's. Finally, there were are few legal cases, such as one involving a book (an "assassination manual") published by Paladin Press and another involving NAMBLA, as to whether publishers or even ISP's could be held to civil liability when unstable individuals commit crimes based on material that these companies have published or facilitated.

Of course, the media has always focused upon computer conduct within the workplace, the legal fact that employees do not have privacy, and that employers may monitor emails and web activity on their servers. But it is clear that in the age of the Internet that off-duty activities have a greater potential to affect employers than was the case previously.

At this point, it is well to note that there had been some level of possible risk from my activities for some time, even if they had gone unnoticed. For example, the book contained many short quotes from other sources. Under the doctrine of copyright "fair use," explicit permission probably was not needed (the fair use doctrine is weaker in for-profit publishing), although it would have required only one aggrieved party to bring a suit and challenge the fair use assumption. Under current law, any printer or distributor or bookstore could have been held liable, although few people in the book business seem to take this remote possibility of trouble seriously.

Another possibility could have been that the website keeps alive the names of individuals (particularly those associated with gays in the military or other gay issues) who might rather let the issue pass (as it would if their names appeared only in print). I have actually had one request to remove one person's name (and that person is obscure) from the website. Still another, at least in theory, is privacy law violation, if a person owning his own business has access to customer lists such as USPS NCOA materials (and might have a publicly known incentive to misuse them).

Furthermore, a self-owned business and associated web domain brings up the possibility of trademark problems, particularly since web domains are available world wide and a business owner like myself may not know about a similarly named business that existed before the days of the Internet. A home-business owner with a sudden global reach will probably not be willing to incur the time and expense of registering his assumed business name in every state and country. There have already been a few cases like this, and this issue doesn't get mentioned much in books about self-publishing. One could propose that self-publishing domains should be named after the individual author and not "fool" the public by imitating corporate names; such a concept is being implement by ICANN with the new ".biz" top-leve-domain suffix.

There was another proposal to trademark the book title phrase "Do Ask Do Tell" for t-shirts and promotional materials but this application was abandoned. (The same word-mark can be used for different categories of products and books may be trademarked only when in a series.)

Even another concern could be zoning. Generally in the telecommuting age writers have been left alone but in New Jersey freelance writers have been pursued and fined, on the theory that they are cheating or denying property owners commercial rent. Many other businesses (such as food preparation) do have strict commercial zoning requirements so writing is just off the radar screen

Finally, small business computer users have a responsibility to master security technology, such as with the proper use of firewalls and anti-virus tools, or they may endanger other interests downstream. The U.S. Patriot Act of 2002 provides stiff civil and even criminal penalties for web server operators (some of whom may have home servers) who allow their sites to be used as "zombies" to attack other corporate of government infrastructures. Conceivably, a controversial writer could attract the attention of heckling terrorists, and provide a measure of risk to those associated with him, and cause him to be perceived as nuisance. My own site, in a passage discussing possible terrorist motives, has been hacked once.

For employers, as already noted, there could be two concerns. One might be that someone who is starting a writing career while still working in a professional capacity might be tempted to misuse information that he learned in the workplace to make a political argument. This opportunity could allow possible compromise of confidential information about other stakeholders, or at least the "appearance" of compromise. This circumstance might sound hard to judge; if a person has a home-based business but access to names and addresses, does that mean that the public (or a regulatory agency) would presume that the person has an incentive to misuse his access to make mailing lists? I can say that I have *never* used confidential data for my own purposes.

For employers, the second concern would mainly be that my reputation could prove distracting to other associates or stakeholders. In discussing such matters that follow from my "conservative" approach to gay rights, issues such as the tension in the workplace between those with families to support and singletons like me, I would run the risk of dragging in people who know or work with me. Therefore, I feel, if I want to continue self-publishing politically controversial material while still working, I should follow certain rules, which are covered in the attached appendix.

The most important rules are that I not have direct reports, not make discretionary decisions that directly affect stakeholders, and that I not speak publicly for the employer (or have my named used conspicuously on a company website or correspondence, as is often done particularly with smaller companies). However, this code of ethics does present some career issues. I would be less valuable to an employer if I was not available for promotion if needed or to represent the company's interests publicly. I would be contained within the opportunities of short-term practical "geek" contracts, and this is becoming increasingly difficult as technology changes so rapidly that maintaining sufficient expertise to make a living working just "behind the throne" is becoming more difficult.

Again, employers have been evasive about the issue of intrusion into "sharp-edged" outside activities and tend to follow a "don't ask, don't tell" paradigm. But some employers have no-moonlighting policies (and it is arguable whether these policies would refer to working at home with self-owned businesses), and many more have non-compete clauses that can be enforced even after termination. Some do try to force employees to sign intellectual property ownership agreements with so-called "grab" clauses. (Note, however, that federal copyright law concerning **work-for-hire** specifically says that employees own work that they do at home with their own resources, even when they are salaried by an employer.) Given that the Internet can make anyone a celebrity, will employers gradually decide that this is an area of an associate's life that they should own, or will they make it standard policy to review this part of a person's work as part of typical professional employment screening process?

This brings up a major point about how people typically advance in the workplace: by advancing and selling the ideas of others. Non-profit pressure groups take this idea and telescope it, asking constituencies to mass email or fax pre-written letters to politicians about some very specific issue that affects their constituencies. I am particularly unwilling to take a job that is predicated on publicly advancing the ideas of others, or of withdrawing my own writings from public availability and leaving the debate to "the establishment." This behavior contradicts the temperament of the artist or creative writer who wants to sell his own ideas. Even so, there is tension and controversy within the literary world between creative writing and work for hire.

Some writers look at writing as a self-defining profession, invoking services that can be marketed guerilla-style to others. This occupation can take on various forms, such as grant writing, where there can be controversy over whether the writing is simply providing technical skill or is supposed to be publicly involved in the fund-raising. The National Writers Union (which sounds to the novice like an oxymoron, a union of freelancers, but more about that when we talk about film) has advocated the idea of a minimum charge of a dollar per word and re-use rights.

All right, there is tension between writers who work strictly for hire and those (like myself) who start out by offering their work, particularly fiction, poetry or editorial content at below-market prices while having income from other sources (especially working in a salaried capacity but intending a second career after "retirement"). Many writers do a mixture of both, but they may feel that they must become established professionally (say as journalists or in academics) before trying to sell their own material. Some older writers believe that they must gain recognition first by getting published with material "that other people want," even to the point of manufacturing formula genre fiction.

This brings up the question, again, about the legitimacy of self-publishing. Should a work have public recognition only when it is funded a third party or when it generates enough revenue to support the author without other income through work? That seems to be how some writers feel. Of course, to get there the writers would have to pay their dues as journalists or by publicly advocating the work of others before they advocate their own views and ideas, and it is that notion that is so disturbing to me.

And the insurance industry seems to take this position. The National Writers Union has tried to offer low-cost group media perils insurance to freelance writers. In 2001, it ran into a roadblock when the underwriting syndicate refused to insure some writers, including me. Actually, the insurance form asked about the amount of third-party legal supervision, which would seem to exclude self-published writers without a lot of resources but NWU insisted that the insurance could be available for self-published writers as well as writing collectives.

In my case, I thought that my involvement in the COPA litigation (that is, putatively "adult" materials) or the age of my books might have caused the declination. But the underwriter wrote back in an email to me, in bald-faced fashion: "They cited the controversial nature of your writings as the reason for the declination." In other words, "f__ you, we don't approve of what you are trying to do, and you know it." Later, NWU discovered that particularly writers of gay and lesbian materials were singled out for declination. Right now, NWU does not have a media perils policy (it may have one soon), and admittedly there is some tension among the writers that the controversy stirred by some could affect the livelihoods of everyone.

Could this spill into the regular workplace? Independent contractors generally must carry their own professional liability insurance but this is usually sold without media perils coverage. Suppliers of contract W-2 employees usually provide this insurance. If one of these contract employees also writes freelance without insurance on his own, could this provide a risk for the "Kelly girl" employer? Probably not, because the law generally recognizes that a person own his own intellectual property if he creates it with his own resources. (Although work-for-hire provisions in federal copyright law are very explicit about this protection, with software in the object-oriented area it is clear that there can be ambiguities.)

However, the litigious nature of our system may eventually make some employers squeamish and this problem underscores the need for tort reform to punish frivolous lawsuits. Another interesting point concerns umbrella insurance, often available from auto or casualty companies. This is not supposed to cover business liability, yet the coverage is excluded for "professional athletes and entertainers." But in the age of the Internet and broadband, who is regarded as an "entertainer?" (Even I get special attention when I eat at Bryant Lake Bowl!)

This brings to the next logical area for writers: film and video. Independent film, traditionally the area for more original and "visionary" content, is in some-sense like self-publishing, although usually venture capitalists and investors do not have a lot of contact with artistic or production decisions (they usually do know about casting choices before they invest). Selling screenplays to mainstream movie production companies is even more difficult than selling novels, as the movies use a system of agents who are even more turf-protective than in the book world.

However, some studios are beginning to develop initiatives to attract truly original material, and have developed software tools to help evaluate screenplays and treatments. Film festivals (especially Sundance, Toronto, and Cannes) have become a major vehicle for independent films to sell to worldwide distributors. (In film, the processes of production and distribution are sometimes more separated than in the book world.) While some people have criticized the festivals as a vehicle for the well-established, others maintain that the festivals welcome truly original material and that really remarkable films will find distribution. The acting and screenwriting guilds (SAG and SGA) seem to be willing to work with independent or low-budget film-makers at greatly reduced rates.

There is in film-writing an especially double-edged controversy over "creativity." People compete fiercely for screenwriting contracts and then relish hidden opportunities to shine when writing scripts according to very detailed directions, especially for television or commercials. There is a continuum been writing to complete another person's concept to writing one's own content and then trying to sell it. However, even in commercials there are sometimes opportunities to present conceptual content, as in the Dell ad where Steven comically outlines the various modes of salesmanship (from groveling to logic) in raising money.

The recent string of corporate scandals, particularly those having to do with conflicts of interest among investment banking, consulting, accounting and auditing activities, raise at least a knee-jerk question for self-publishers. Should "Chinese walls" exist between authorship, publication and distribution in order to guarantee professionalism and provide supervision to those like myself who provide information to the public for present recognition and future financial or career gains? Self-publishing websites boldly encourage new authors to self-publish inexpensively now, whereas (as of this writing) groups like the Authors' Guild restrict membership mainly to writers able to gain advances against royalties from established commercial (and university) publishers (including periodicals). (It does offer associate memberships for pending contracts with trade publishers. Nevertheless, the Authors' Guild has not yet, as of this writing in mid 2002, offered group media perils insurance either.) Would the Guild be open to considering self-published or cooperatively published books as qualifying if publicly audited sales volume or operational profits met prescribed targets within a specified time period after publication? Even so, public recognition does and effectiveness in stimulating debate does not always correlate to money.

There are significant differences between the potential collusions in publishing and film-making as compared to other businesses. Self-published authors often use their own money and when they do use investors these outside sources often do screen them carefully. Furthermore, the breakdown in corporate America seems to be largely a total failure in the self-regulatory and auditing processes that supposedly had been set up to provide supervision. When external entities can control what is published or broadcast, there is not only a compromise to free speech but there are also opportunities for corruption as with the Payola scandals in the music industry back in the 1950s. Some left-wing sources maintain that unregulated mergers among ISP's and cable companies will eventually squash personal and small-business websites and self-publishing. Aggressive efforts by music and entertainment companies to protect their intellectual property rights (especially from downloading and copying of their works, as copyright infringement) may interfere with future deployments of home personal computer technology that would otherwise creating works (especially media and multi-media) for self-publishing.

One could postulate that self-publishing should justify itself with financial results, if made publicly available. Along those lines, one wonders if the companies offering self-publishing or cooperative publishing services will be profitable enough to continue offering their opportunities indefinitely, or if they will have to become more selective in what they publish (even given that print-on-demand erases inventories). Likewise, will e-commerce sites keep indefinitely database entries for items that do not sell? On the other hand, some e-commerce sites have been criticized for "undermining" authors and publishers by auctioning used books, but even the auctions keep the books listed. Should e-commerce sites identify books as to mode of publication? To date, the Library of Congress and Books In Print have listed self-published books without restriction, although print-on-demand is listed by Books in Print only on CD-rom for purchase by libraries. However, apparently some major book distributors are no longer accepting self-published books, at least from "one book" publishers. Although many self-published and cooperatively published are of well done (and although many trade royalty publishers are putting more responsibilities back onto authors, maintaining the notorious indemnification clauses in their publishing contracts while reducing their willingness to provide writers legal help and supervision), the public may be mislead when it sees a book on an e-commerce site and has no idea how it was published, or when it sees ".com" as a domain name and cannot tell if there is a real going concern business behind the site.

Indeed, I may, with my writings, have competed with organizations (in the gay and libertarian areas) that I support, and have complicated their messages—but the complicated arguments about these social issues need to be exhibited completely. Or, I may simply be sidestepping committed support and participating because of competition for my own time and resources. For me to be credible, I normally cannot allow myself to speak publicly on behalf of another organization or to represent the organization with my own name and identity.

The ethical issues possibly associated with self-publishing derive from the lack of societal experience with a new and inexpensive medium for self-promotion (as Clive Barker calls it in his sensational novel *Sacrament*, or, to put it baldly, drawing attention to oneself with "truth"). Various paradigms of how people perceive right and wrong in this area can evolve, but already it seems that the potential for good (new speech) is great and that, given the relatively small financial investments involved, the potential for harm (turf erosion, unwanted publicity and possibly incidental exposure to children) is much less than for other developments associated with the Internet, such as conflicts of interest in the brokerage and financial services industries, scams, and child pornography.

Some people, of course, are put off by the idea of public "self-promotion" even if this has been encouraged by the go-go attitudes of the past decade. From a personal perspective, self-publishing and the resulting publicity have given me considerable practical social respectability in a gay community for which aging otherwise presents difficult problems of often feeling unwelcome around younger people; this observation makes the moral questions particularly pungent.

So the whole issue of self-publishing and perhaps self-promotion pits two trends against one another: entrepreneurialism and innovation on the one hand, and professionalism and paying your dues on the other. As tested recently in the Seattle area when a public housing participant was jailed for refusing to remove privileged information from his own website, the self-publishing explosion will raise the question as to whether there really does exist a "fundamental right to publish" apart from clearly established rights for private speech, expressive association, and of freedom of the press. It is time that the reading and writing public take note of this "investiture" controversy, and hopefully the public will reverse the course of its past squeamishness about politically incorrect speech and weigh the democratic importance of free speech heavily as unforeseen complications develop. Self-publishing of controversial materials does result in a self-embedded tattoo and brings up, in the minds of some people, some ethical gray zones, but it's time to recognize these.

Scale and repetition, usually necessary in business for operational profits, run counter to the intellectual originality so tied to free speech and so important to our democratic political traditions. Yet to be taken seriously any speaker ought to be accountable for what he or she published, ought to establish authenticity, and ought to live up to his or her own teachings. But probably the ultimate judge of the ethics of a new writer like me in this uncertain area has to be common sense. Only the pattern and consistency of ethical conduct over time can give a writer's customers confidence that the writer will not abuse trust.

10:

THE CHILD ONLINE PROTECTION ACT OF 1998 WOULD SUPPRESS FREE SPEECH AMONG ADULTS

In June 1997, the Supreme Court overturned many provisions of the Communications Decency Act, those measures in the law that would have effectively prohibited "indecent" (though not "obscene") postings on the Internet in any area publicly accessible to minors. The CDA had even made certain subject matter (as having to do with promoting abortion) indecent for the purposes of the law. The Court held that much of the Act was overbroad and that it unreasonably and unnecessarily burdened legal communication between adults as protected by the First Amendment. Although this is not generally known, some provisions of the CDA actually promoted free speech and were left intact. For example, it contains a provision to protect Internet service providers from liability if their customer websites post illegal content, although today there may be some exceptions (such as potential ISP downstream liability associated with the Patriot Act as well as a few suits against ISP's that allegedly may have knowingly hosted particularly violent content).

In October 1998, Congress tried to remedy this constitutional defect with the Child Online Protection Act ("COPA" or "CDA II"). The law is limited in application to commercial sites (those with anything at all to sell) and it replaces the notion of indecency with the nebulous "harmful to minors" standard. "Harmful to minors" essentially means "obscene with respect to minors." A "commercial" posting available to minors (of any age under 17) is unlawful if an "average person" would find the web page patently offensive or prurient with respect to minors and without redeeming value with respect to minors (that is, presumably all minors). Apparently, non-pornographic adult material or subject matter could be found harmful to minors. An affirmative defense is secured by requiring credit card access or adult verification for any online file having such materials. The law did not deal specifically with violent material, and it did (somewhat clumsily) try to exempt Internet service providers from liability for the crimes of their customers.

The law defined "harmful to minors" with a list of three prongs, which essentially enumerated as follows: (1) appealing to the prurient interest of minors; (2) sexually explicit, either with graphics or detailed written description or possibly even by reference and inference (the law did mention the post-pubescent female breast); (3) not having serious literary, social, political or scientific value for minors. Content apparently would meet the legal definition of "harmful to minors" only if it satisfied all three prongs. The law used the notion of community standards borrowed from the well-known custom with obscenity.

In November 1998, a coalition of seventeen plaintiffs filed suit in federal court to have the law overturned. As a member of Electronic Frontier Foundation, I am named as an "indirect plaintiff." I had authored my ambitious book, *Do Ask, Do Tell*, about libertarianism and gay rights, which I maintain with supporting materials at my site, hppub.com, and some of my material is moderately adult in subject matter. For me, requiring credit-card or other viewer-identifying adult access to see my materials would have been totally impractical and would have shut down or discouraged much traffic to my site, even if I could afford to implement a credit-card facility.

The law appears to have been motivated by pre-election posturing, particularly to impress voters that Congress would protect children. In fact the law does little to shield children from inappropriate materials. Most hard-core pornography on the web already requires credit card or adult access, although some operators "tease" consumers with free "previews" (the Justice Department has maintained that stopping this was the "real" intention behind COPA, however clumsily and laboriously worded).

More significant is that (even given technology as of the time of passage in 1998), parents already have several effective ways to keep adult materials from their kids, all of these established voluntarily by private Internet service companies for their customers. They can choose ISP's that offer kids' accounts with limited access to a predefined list of "G-rated" sites approved by their ISP's. More recently, some ISP's such as AOL have offered several ages ranges for minors with appropriate predefined content for each range (in a manner analogous to movie ratings). With only a little computer knowledge, parents may set their browsers to accept only sites rated to specific levels as to adult content (according to the Platform for Internet Content Selection). Or they may install one of several screening programs that inspect all sites for objectionable material.

There have been cases where children and young teens have discovered grossly indecent materials, *but in practically every such case the parents had failed to install controls.* Furthermore, all reputable service providers have codes of conduct (such as AOL's "Terms of Service") which are much more understandable and reasonable than laws like CDA or COPA. Then, one should ask Congress, why is COPA necessary?

Arguably, commercial operators may have some responsibility to protect the public from their products regardless of what parents do. Yet the "affirmative defenses" proposed by Congress would (without much affecting commercial pornography) effectively hamper access to free content and circulation of lively discussion about important issues, both personal (such as safer sex) and public.

The web has become an effective way to present difficult materials with more depth than used to be possible. In the past, political issues about sensitive moral questions tended to be aired in a polarized fashion and to be settled by taking sides, raising money and counting votes while airing the simplest (and most emotional) rhetoric possible. Some problems, such as public health, gays in the military, and recently the conduct of our president, require delving into adult concepts before they can be understood in depth. Individuals and small businesses with intellectual property to "sell" can, by presenting these issues, often counter (and perhaps undermine) well-funded political organizations, certainly with more effectiveness than individuals simply venting personal opinions with letters to editors and or venting sentiments with pre-written broadcast faxes to public officials.

COPA, while perhaps intended by some lawmakers merely to stop commercial pornographers from "advertising" indecent exposures in public, may be taken in some communities as a warrant to stop all adult discussions on the Internet within possible sight of children. If certain things are right or wrong, then, according to some people, they just don't need to be discussed in public. Leave that to the pastors and professionals! Of course, this attitude does run counter to the First Amendment.

COPA indeed brings up the "cultural war" hedge issue: How much freedom should adults sacrifice to protect children from inadvertent harm? It also invokes the question, whether people should expect simple answers to difficult cultural questions (as through religion) or should work out tough issues on their own. (And, yes, I wonder whether the Minnesota Profiles in Learning would ultimately stunt the ability of people to look at issues on their own.)

On February 1, 1999, Judge Lowell Reed of the Eastern District of Pennsylvania issued a Preliminary Injunction prohibiting the Justice Department from enforcing COPA. In the early passages in his Opinion he writes that the Internet has taken much of the power to influence public opinion out of the hands of the corporate owners of the press and placed it in the hands of individuals with moderate means but definitely valuable messages to publish. Indeed, the technological changes of the past fifteen years have emphasized economies of scale in some industries but individualism and entrepreneurialism in others. The opportunity to publish valuable, provocative materials without bureaucratic supervision and without the approval of others is surely controversial to some people who make see information as a consumer good that should be regulated.

COPA is not the only threat to this. Some will call for holding authors, publishers or Internet service providers responsible when others use their writings or facilities to commit crimes (whether securities fraud or murder), and thereby keep the right to influence public opinion or achieve in the creative arenas under the control of politicians or other vested interests. For example, there is a lawsuit (settled out of court in 2001) against the author and publisher of an "assassination manual" over a crime committed by someone who apparently followed its recipe closely.

On April 2, 1999 the Justice Department appealed this injunction to the Third Circuit Court of Appeals in Philadelphia. The Appeals Court upheld the injunction in June 2000, with an argument that focused particularly upon the topology of the Internet. The Court held essentially that the application of community standards would make the law unconstitutional, because it would place the most conservative communities in the nation in a position to heckle materials off of the open Internet for mainstream and liberal communities.

In June 2001 the Supreme Court accepted an appeal from the Justice Department. On the surface, it appeared that the Court might review all of the different levels of concern over the implications of a law like this for the First Amendment. Soon, however, it was clear that the Court's greatest concern was the particular rationale offered by the Third Circuit. If COPA could be invalidated because of the failure of community standards, then a whole body of obscenity law might also be at risk.

The Justice Department wrote energetic briefs that downplayed the potential harm done by use of community standards. It invoked several important cases, such as Miller,[86] Hamling,[87] and Sable.[88] The "serious value" or third prong, it argued, had always been understood, even in obscenity law, to refer to a national standard. Furthermore it conceded that the serious value clause could be invoked if material has value "for a legitimate minority of older minors." In informal terms, this means that material that was valuable for mature teens like the fictional characters Clark Kent (*Smallville*), Peter Parker (*Spider Man*) or maybe even Harry Potter would be acceptable.

As for the other two prongs, the definitions were clear enough, in its view, so that only pornography (possibly of the soft-core Playboy variety) could be affected. The separation of quasi-pornography by an "electronic brown wrapper" would be comparable to keeping such material in separate adults-only sections of convenience stores or gay book stores. Since most of the plaintiffs (myself included) offered adult but putatively non-pornographic materials, we (as plaintiffs) likely did not have standing to sue, according to this theory.

Oral arguments took place on November 28, 2001, about eleven weeks after 9-11 and, I will add, on the fortieth anniversary of my undignified expulsion from the College of William and Mary. The Court in posing ad hoc questions did show appropriate concern that a conservative community could essentially mediate the Internet for everyone. But it (particularly in the comments by Justice Breyer) also proposed the idea of a national community standard. It further gave credibility to the idea that a jury could be instructed to apply a national standard (for all of the prongs) rather than the particular standards of the specific geographic communities that the jurors may have come from.

On the other hand, the ACLU pointed out that the use of a national standard still could deny adults ready access to constitutionally protected materials, a situation different from that with obscenity law. One controversy that developed during the hearings was how many of the plaintiffs really could be at risk of prosecution. The government seemed to think that there were only three such plaintiffs. The ACLU pointed out that the threshold for application of "harmful to minors" definition could change at government whim, and that therefore there would exist a "chilling effect" on speech.

The Supreme Court ruled on May 13, 2001 (ironically while I had traveled back to Washington). It vacated the Third Circuit's opinion but left the injunction in place. It instructed the Third Circuit to rule on whether COPA, given the troubling questions about the mechanics of how it could actually work, would pass the least intrusive means tests required by First Amendment strict scrutiny. However, it did hold that the application of community standards would not by itself render the statute unconstitutional.

The Court's opinion did show considerable respect for the content of a number of the sites, some of which (like mine) had proportionally only a small volume of material that might be viewed as harmful to minors but for whom this material was a critical component to what the publishers or authors had to say. It also paid some attention to the questions over what is a commercial provider, particularly if that is an individual self-publishing political materials through a home-based business and not intending to sell pornography.

But Justice Thomas, in a statement that was not concurred by other justices, suggested (based on Hamling and Sable) that publishers of harmful to minors materials should merely use publishing mechanisms (that is, mail or other hardcopy delivery) that permit them to physically sieve different materials for different destinations (that is, that the Internet was not a legitimate means to publish harmful to minors literature commercially at all). To quote: "If a publisher chooses to send its material into a particular community, this Courts jurisprudence teaches that it is the publisher's responsibility to abide by that community's standards. The publisher's burden does not change simply because it decides to distribute its material to every community in the Nation." Justice Thomas's comment would sound like an invitation for a state or locality do define "harmful to minors" very broadly to heckle out Internet traffic, but the Court concurred that case law establishes a national standard for at least the "serious value" prong.

Here, I want to back up and reiterate my basic concern, as expressed in my affidavit, of how COPA might have affected a "new man in the block" of creative or controversial Internet writing and self-publishing. The sum of my argument depends upon presenting some material having particularly to do with male homosexuality and the way a segment of society views homosexuality as "cheating the system," that is frankly mature in nature, probably suitable (even important) for high school teens but not for young minors, who might view such material as sensational or prurient. Since I am self-publishing with my own money and limited resources, a prosecutor and jury might view me as promoting myself in front of children. An important component of my strategy is the offering of most of the material for free on the Internet to attract readers ("passive advertising" as opposed to "guerilla marketing"), as well as to offer hardcopy for sale through the Internet and retail outlets. It would be possible to maintain several arguments.

First, should not material available to minors be segregated in a way similar to movie ratings? (My material, if filmed, would probably correspond to the R rating.) Second, if I want commercial gain, should I not be expected to have the scale that would protect children even from moderately adult materials? In late 2000 I discussed all of this with a reported at the Minneapolis *Star Tribune*, and she asked me why I should not be expected to make a (mutually exclusive) choice between print only, or totally non-commercial free Internet content without books to sell. Why, she asked, would this not satisfy First Amendment concerns?

One possible answer is that commercial speech does have considerable protection in prior case law, and a commercial component often enhances the reach, political effectiveness, and public credibility of an individual's speech. Another possibility is that some communities might view some kinds of subject matter, especially gay-related materials, as prurient with respect to minors by definition. The ACLU raised this possibility in briefs, with mention of the military "don't ask don't tell" policy in one place (possibly because of prodding by me—and I'll add here that I'm pretty sure that the legal clerks in the Supreme Court read all of the legal theories about DADT in my writings, as if I had succeeded in getting the DADT question before the Court in a case that it would actually take). And end result could be, in theory, that it could be illegal to advertise any gay-related product for sale on the Internet.

Nevertheless and in the second place, it is possible to read the text of the harmful to minors definitions as being particularly focused upon sexual acts or sexual parts themselves (particularly with the Second Prong) and if so, categorical material like general discussions of homosexuality would not fall into concern (even ignoring the community standards problem) until the speaker became specific with respect to sexual activity itself (as with conveying safer sex information). The Court shows some concern over the possibility that this would not be the case, as when it mentions discussions of gay parents. Another important concern is that, as a practical matter, the government could use civil lawsuits rather than criminal prosecution to harass speakers when the government believed that only a lower standard of proof, often based on the sympathy of a jury, was achievable.

But, in the third place, this would lead to what the Third Circuit must take up now, the least restrictive means analysis, and the effectiveness of various schemes to separate young minors from adult content. The Supreme Court, in the oral arguments, asked if a self-rating system attached to browsers was feasible. The ACLU responded that this would not be possible for small Internet content providers like myself, but that assertion is not correct.

The Internet Content Rating Association, for example, is developing a scheme to label web pages with meta-tags, and then parents will be able to configure browsers and ISP services like AOL to block content that has been self-rated in various ways (and the ICRA acts as a third party to corroborate the self-ratings and give them credibility). This is inherently inexpensive for individuals and small businesses, although it may require more software development by browser developers such as Microsoft.

A more advanced method might be to place adult-like material into XML pages (rather than native HTML), maybe dumped off a relational knowledge database, and then use parsers, schemas and style sheets (associated with the java or similar object-oriented programming language or with other facilities offered, for example, by Microsoft .NET) to filter out content elements according to the profile of the viewer (again, parents would have some responsibility to set this up) and the geographical location of the viewer (considering some kind of artificial intelligence profile for the community standards for that location).[89] Software companies would be able to develop and refine such a mechanism if they perceived an economic payoff according to the final legal disposition of this issue. Perhaps geographical sensitivity could be implemented in newer object-oriented languages as interfaces.

As for credit cards and adult-ID services, the ACLU rather than the government is certainly right. Credit cards are only suitable for sites with large transaction volumes, not for content providers who offload their merchant processing to places like Amazon or Barnes and Noble. And so far adult-ID companies have been offering services only for viewing outright pornography, not for educational adult content. But there is no reason why venture capitalists could not come up with a new style for adult-id services, if the market for them was there.

There are several other pieces of legislation that are sometimes confused with COPA. For example, a Children's Internet Protection Act (CIPA) effective 2001, would require schools and libraries getting federal funds to install filters for pornography and adult material. This is less draconian than CDA or COPA but still involves government-sponsored censorship, using technology that cannot reliably separate pornography from adult non-pornographic (and First Amendment protected) material. Accordingly, the Third Circuit struck down this law in May 2002 in an opinion that acknowledged an imperfect world and that, given the limited technological reliability of filters with non-pornographic adult content, it would be impermissible to interfere with the communication of some intellectually legitimate ideas to minors because of the imperfections of technology. Unclear is whether filtering only some computers in a children's room might be legally acceptable, whatever common sense tells us.

There is also a Children's Online Privacy Protection Act (COPPA, 1998) associated with COPA, and this merely prohibits web sites from collection information it knows to be children under thirteen without consent of parents. This provision has not been challenged.

Also in 1995, Congress considered making it a crime (at least in pictures) to suggest that a minor is engaging in sexual activity even if an adult is used or the viewable image is generated by computer. Remember the film *The Tin Drum*, which a district attorney in Oklahoma tried to ban on the theory that a particular bedroom scene constitutes child pornography. Congress passed the Child Pornography Prevention Act (CPPA) in 1996. On February 12, 2001, ABC "Nightline" covered this problem thoroughly. The Act provides that material (on the Internet, in books, or in film) which "looks like" child pornography (that is, virtual child pornography) is prosecutable even if no child is used to produce it. Specifically, in the language of the statute, "'child pornography' means any visual depiction, including any photograph, film, video, picture, drawing, or computer or computer-generated image or picture, whether made or produced by electronic, mechanical, or other means, of sexually explicit conduct, where—

(A) the production of such visual depiction involves the use of a minor engaging in sexually explicit conduct;

(B) such visual depiction is, or appears to be, of a minor engaging in sexually explicit conduct; or

(C) such visual depiction is advertised, promoted, presented, described, or distributed in such a manner that conveys the impression that the material is or contains a visual depiction of a minor engaging in sexually explicit conduct." [90]

The book *Lolita*, which describes a love affair with a twelve-year-old girl, might be illegal. What about a novel that describes a sex act with a person underage in some states even if (in the fictionalized setting) the person looks like an adult or the character committing the crime in the plot of the novel does not know that the person is underage (an interesting pretext for a novel)? Is all of this "thoughtcrime"? What about sex education materials? Is there a principled distinction between cartoons and virtual reality depictions of sex acts? Of course, many will argue that computer generated images of children in sex acts encourages (by "mental effects") actual sex acts against children by unstable people. This law has some of the problems of COPA. (Below is a good reference on this Act: http://www.parrhesia.com/cp.html. It would appear from this analysis that an affirmative defense is provided if the speaker or distributor does not advertise the material as portraying sex by minors and if real adult actors are used. However, Jerry Hall of Tate & Bywater raises troubling questions about state jurisdiction at http://www.tatebywater.com/features/099705.html.) The Supreme Court heard oral arguments on this, Ashcroft v. Free Speech Coalition, 00-795, on Oct. 29, 2001. See http://www.cnn.com/2001/LAW/10/30/scotus.child.porn.ap/index.html . The movie *Traffic* was mentioned, and I know of others that could conceivably be affected by the law (such as the thriller *The Deep End*).

On April 16, 2002, The Supreme Court overturned this law, voting 6-3. Justice Anthony Kennedy, writing for the majority, said, "The mere tendency of speech to encourage unlawful acts is not a sufficient reason for banning it. The right to think is the beginning of freedom and speech must be protected from government because speech is the beginning of thought."

It is well to note here that the federal government has recently become very aggressive in pursuing child pornography customers, to the point of setting up stings (such as "Candyman" in early 2002) and then obtaining search warrants to examine the hard drives of customers for cached or deleted images. Possession of child pornography is a strict liability offense much like drug possession, so even clicking upon an image that one knows to be child pornography is considered a crime. Persons caught in these dragnets generally have no criminal records and have been "guilty" only of idle or inappropriate curiosity.[91] It is easy to imagine how such enforcement efforts could someday ensnare persons who may have illegal images on their hard drives without their awareness.

The most important issue for me, in looking at COPA and similar legislation intended to protect children, goes deeper than just hindering access of adults to constitutionally protected materials. It raises the question as to whether certain conventional ideas (particularly those grounded in religious faith), because they are more acceptable to an "average person," will achieve more attention in public debate than will more daring and challenging notions. The possibility of individuals and small business or political interests to widely disseminate their ideas, at some possible risk to younger children who may be inadvertently exposed to material over their heads, does tend to level political debate in the long run.

This article appeared in the *Minnesota Libertarian*, July 1998, page 6, but has been brought up to date.[92]

APPENDIX 1:

AFFIDAVIT OF JOHN WILLIAM BOUSHKA IN ACLU v. RENO II, CHALLENGING THE CHILD ONLINE PROTECTION ACT (COPA)

IN THE UNITED STATES DISTRICT COURT FOR THE EASTERN DISTRICT OF PENNSYLVANIA

The plaintiffs are as follows

AMERICAN CIVIL LIBERTIES UNION, A DIFFERENT LIGHT BOOKSTORES, AMERICAN BOOKSELLERS, FOUNDATION FOR FREE EXPRESSION, ASSOCIATION OF AMERICAN PUBLISHERS, ARTNET, BLACKSTRIPE, CONDOMANIA, ELECTRONIC FRONTIER FOUNDATION, ELECTRONIC PRIVACY INFORMATION CENTER, FREE SPEECH MEDIA, INTERNET CONTENT COALITION, OBGYN.NET, PHILADELPHIA GAY NEWS, PLANETOUT, POWELL'S BOOKSTORE, RIOTGRRL, SALON INTERNET, INC. AND WEST STOCK, forCivil Action No. 98-5591

AFFIDAVIT OF JOHN WILLIAM BOUSHKA

I, JOHN WILLIAM BOUSHKA, hereby declare and affirm the following:

1)   I am a member of the Electronic Frontier Foundation.

2)   I am the individual owner of a publishing company called High Productivity Publishing. High Productivity Publishing is a sole proprietorship that was registered in Fairfax County, Virginia, on January 2, 1997. Registration was transferred to Minneapolis, Minnesota, in April of 1998.

3)   I formed High Productivity Publishing to help establish myself as a credible political and social commentator in the area of individual rights and responsibilities. I am hoping to eventually take advantage of writing opportunities with major commercial publishers or even motion picture ventures.

4)   I work as a salaried computer programmer-analyst for a financial institution for a living and run High Productivity Publishing in my spare time. I have spoken publicly on the topic of "don't ask, don't tell" on numerous occasions. I discussed the book and constitutional amendment proposal before an audience of students and libertarian party members at Hamline University. That talk was videotaped and shown several times on Minneapolis-St.Paul public (cable) access.

5)   My first project was to write and publish a non-fiction book entitled, <u>Do Ask, Do Tell: A Gay Conservative Lashes Back</u> (hereinafter "<u>Do Ask, Do Tell</u>", ISBN 0-9656744-0-1), which was published in hard-copy book form in July of 1997.

6)   In <u>Do Ask, Do Tell</u>, I propose an argument and strategy for the overhaul of the Bill of Rights. The book maintains that the American people need to perform, in structured public debates, a systematic study of ways that they should safeguard their individual rights against government intrusion. The book is especially concerned about laws concerning consensual sex, drugs, gambling, civil asset forfeitures, past conscription, government-sponsored racial preferences, discriminatory marriage laws, sodomy laws, gun control, and the tension in the workplace between people with different family responsibilities. The overall political philosophy is a moderate form of libertarianism. I believe that the law should emphasize personal responsibility more, and group rights or status less.

7)   I present my case inductively, with early portions of the book devoted to my own personal experience as a gay man. The fulcrum of the entire argument is the role of the military in society as a whole. My own unusual participation in the debate over gays in the military in 1993 serves as the backdrop of the book. The book takes the position that the damage done to gays by the military ban goes way beyond the military itself.

8)   On August 1, 1998, Professor Mark Wojcik from the John Marshall Law School in Chicago presented a discussion of the ban and of military sodomy laws before a sub-panel of the American Bar Association, a panel comprising mostly senior military officers. My book was given as a significant reference on the legislative and political history of the military gay ban and particularly the Clinton Administration's "don't ask, don't tell" policy.

9)   <u>Do Ask, Do Tell</u> is available through many sources, including Web booksellers amazon.com and barnesandnoble.com. It can also be ordered at Barnes and Noble retail stores throughout the country. The downtown Minneapolis store carries it in stock.

10)   I am currently writing another non-fiction supplemental book entitled, <u>Our Fundamental Rights and How We Can Reclaim Them</u> (ISBN 909656744-2-8). In the future, I plan on writing a major fiction project.

11)   I have created and maintain a site on the World Wide Web for High Productivity Publishing at http://www.hppub.com. The Web site was set up originally to help sell <u>Do Ask, Do Tell</u> and also to provide readers with supplementary material. Very quickly I added many other topical materials to the Web site, mostly short essays or lists about libertarian philosophy, family values, discrimination law, affirmative action, health care, AIDS, marriage law, and more materials on the military's "don't ask, don't tell" policy. I added a special section on psychological growth, which fits into my argument in an unusual way. Recently, I put up a section of book and movie reviews (mostly of adult-oriented books or movies). I even added a little humor, such as a satirical paraphrase of the "don't ask, don't tell" policy entitled, "Heterosexuality Is Incompatible with Military Service," which had been published in 1996 by *The Washington Blade* newspaper. I also post written contributions from readers of the site.

12)   I have added links to external organizations with related materials. These include sites owned by Gays and Lesbians for Individual Liberty (I edit *The Quill*, their newsletter), Servicemembers' Legal Defense Network, the Ninth Street Center, Metropolitan Community Church, and various libertarian groups.

13)   All of the information on my site is available for free to both adults and children. I also sell hard-copies of my book there. The purpose of my site is commercial, to advertise my writings and establish my expertise in this area.

14)   I do not take credit cards at my site, because I cannot afford the setup and access fees the credit verification companies would charge me. When I get an order by e-mail, I simply ask the purchaser to send a check upon receipt of the book under the honor system, and this has worked in practice for me.

15)   For the month of October 1998, my site had almost 700 successful page requests from more than 320 distinct hosts.

16)   On July 31, 1998 (about a year after hard-copy book publication), I posted online at my site the entire text of the <u>Do Ask, Do Tell</u> book (a total of about 187,000 words of text) in six large and several smaller files. All of the files of my book are readable for free with standard Web browsers, such as Netscape or Internet Explorer.

17)   The substance and subject matter of the <u>Do Ask, Do Tell</u> book, as well as some of the essays on my Web site, are definitely adult in content. They require a degree of maturity from the reader. The preface to <u>Do Ask, Do Tell</u> recommends the book for adults and high school teenagers about 15 years of age or older with parental or teacher guidance.

18)   The writing is dense and not easily understood by younger minors. But some concepts, on their face, might be disturbing to immature persons. For example, the feelings that young men have about their bodies and sexual performance is discussed frankly, in setting up a complete understanding of the "unit cohesion" problem later articulated by Sam Nunn and Charles Moskos in the 1993 debate over gays in the military. The idea that some men (homosexual or not) enjoy sexual "submission" is presented and later shown to have political importance.

19)   Furthermore, in the first three chapters of the <u>Do Ask, Do Tell</u> book, there is some graphic language. Most of this occurs when young

men in the dorms or (later) in military barracks are depicted as displaying their (hostile) attitudes towards women and homosexuals. For example, on page 9, the last paragraph reads, "Actually, the boys had brought it up anyway. Just a week ago, there had been another sign on my dorm door, 'Xxxx Xxxx from Golden Genius, 25 cents.' I had quietly taken it down as if it were a Christmas ornament." There is some explicit language in reporting the gay talk groups at the Ninth Street Center (psychological polarities as they relate to sexual identity and to gender identity). And there is explicit language in describing some personal experiences, such as a first visit to a gay bath house (to set up discussion of AIDS later in the book). For example, on page 95, it says: "January 1975, almost two years after my 'second coming,' I finally gained my 'first experience,' at the Club Baths. It was nearly impossible to nightwalk the orgy room, bathed in astral violets, without having at least a passive incident. So what if I were a fallen male!"

20)   There is some explicit discussion of sexual acts in relation to the medical transmissibility of HIV and other infectious agents. Later, there is some discussion of such matters as drugs, abortion, and prostitution.

21)   When I read the exact words of the Child Online Protection Act (the Act), I cannot reassure myself of exactly what is prohibited. The definition of "harmful to minors" seems to me to be self-contradictory or at best ambiguous.

22)   I am concerned that some prosecutor somewhere may want to interpret the Act as applying to all adult subject matter, and therefore to the material on my site. Because of my concerns and my fear of imprisonment or fines, on November 4, 1998, I self-censored the High Productivity Publishing Web site.

23) To self-censor, I replaced the original text of the first three chapters of the online version of the <u>Do Ask, Do Tell</u> book with edited versions of these chapters. In the edited versions, I removed the most "offensive" language and deleted or otherwise toned down the most explicit passages. The affected passages are marked with plus signs ("+"), which are linked to an explanation that to see the original material a reader must either order the printed book (or buy it from a retailer) or contact me for age verification, after which I would provide access. For example, the paragraph from page 9 above has been changed to: "Actually, the boys had brought it up anyway. Just a week ago, there had been another sign on my dorm door ++offering homosexual activity for money+. I had quietly taken it down as if it were a Christmas ornament." The paragraph from page 95 above has been changed to: "January 1975, almost two years after my "second coming," I finally ++experienced sex for the first time at the Club Baths. (omitted sentence) +

24) I saved the original text of the first three chapters in a hidden, password-protected directory (without permissions for normal search engines). These changes took about two hours of my time. When I do provide access, I will do that by giving out the password over the telephone.

25) So far, I have changed only the first three chapters from the book. There are a few essays, particularly in the psychological link (dealing with "polarities") that I will need to look at. There are some older essays from 1996 (an earlier form of the book) that I will want to look at, but these probably do not contain explicit language, just some mildly adult subject matter.

26) I have not edited anyone else' s work (under readers.htm) for adult content. I do not recall coming across anything very explicit, except maybe some technical language about same-sex marriage, etc. But I would

be uncomfortable editing this material anyway. Am I to become a censor under the Act?

27)   So far, no one has called for access. I should also mention that most people who call will get my answering machine, since I work full-time outside of my home on weekdays. In addition, my access telephone number is local only to the Minneapolis-Saint Paul area and would be a toll call users everywhere else. Because of these limitations, I do not expect many people to actually take advantage of my age verification procedure, meaning that even adults will be precluded from accessing my materials.

28)   My site is very small, and I know it intimately since I am both the content author and site maintainer. It would have been much more difficult, if not impossible, for me to self-censor if my site had been more extensive. Setting up alternative, password-protected directories is not a feasible solution for a site with hundreds of materials that would require shielding. It took me two hours to make the changes required of me under the Act to my little site, and it will take me additional time to verify the age of individuals who do want to access the adult materials on my site.

29)   My age verification plans are hardly failsafe. When someone wants access to the original text, I plan on doing a telephone interview, asking the person questions to make it credible that he or she is 17 or older. For example, a student in college or in graduate school or working in a reasonably professional job is not likely to be under 17. This in itself is not costly (other than my time). But it is risky; in that a person could pose as an imposter to determine if I would actually sell to a minor under 17. Adding this barrier to access is also quite likely to deter adults from viewing the original text.

30)   Furthermore, I have only moderate confidence that my self-censorship complies with the law. The text of <u>Do Ask, Do Tell</u> is very long,

and there are many passages with borderline "adult language" which I did not self-censor. For example, on page 19 of the text, it says: "Furthermore, male homosexual sex, they claimed, was qualitatively even more dangerous to "society" than (multiple partner) vaginal sex because, first, the rectum (and perhaps mouth) were more easily damaged in intercourse (because of lack of lubrication and thinner rectal wall, making minor tears more likely) and, even more important, because among male homosexuals, the same individual who "receives" can turn around and "give," and propagate a chain letter or pyramid of easy transmission. (At least with vaginal sex, the difficulty of transmission from female to male, when there are not other diseases around to facilitate transmission, putatively makes sustaining a long chain of infection less likely; this analogy does not hold with true "venereal," as opposed to sexually transmitted, diseases like herpes and venereal warts.)

31)   In addition, in the appendix (the file append.htm) I reproduce the entire text of a draconian bill (HR 2138) proposed in the Texas legislature in 1983 to "strengthen" the state sodomy law during the historical height of public AIDS hysteria. The text is very graphic, but presumably, because it was a proposed state statute, it has redeeming political value even for minors; but I am not sure how I can determine that.

32)   Even though the writing is certainly not as effective when toned down, I plan to leave the site in this censored format at least until there is a permanent injunction against enforcement of the Act.

33)   Forced age verification will discourage traffic at a site like mine, where I am trying, over a long period of time, to establish myself. I have heard from news reports and know from own squeamishness that even adults will be uncomfortable giving credit card numbers or verification codes to do brief searches of files for research, which I think they might want to do with my <u>Do Ask, Do Tell</u> book and other materials.

Furthermore, one of the reasons the World Wide Web is so popular for materials like mine is that people can access them anonymously. My users will not want me, or anyone else, to know they have accessed my or any other adult-subject site.

34)   I have, however, contacted both validate.com and adultpass.com about setting up an age verification system on portions of my site. Validate.com and adultpass.com are Internet-based companies that sell adult verification numbers to consumers for up to $19.95 a year or $29.95 for 2 years. These numbers are supposed to enable adults to log in to "adult" sites that already require verification. I have personally obtained IDs from both companies, but I have not tried to use them to dial into porn sites yet; I only applied to see how the process works. So far, I have heard no response from either company. I do not know how much they would charge. I think they do not believe that non-pornographic, text-only sites need register with them.

35)   My motive in signing up was to find out how the process of adult validation works today. One site (adultpass) required a credit card for membership. The second required that I send in a check and photocopy my Minnesota Driver's License. Both companies advertised a long list of "adult sites" that appeared to be explicitly pornographic in nature (both gay and straight). It did not appear that any of the advertised sites contained political or social discussions. My impression of the adult validation industry is that it is not presently prepared for a large number of small sites with marginally adult or HTM content from operators who want to sign up merely because of fear of prosecution and not really to sell pornographic materials. There may be an audience of consumers who willingly use credit cards and adult verification numbers for the purpose of purchasing large amounts of entertainment pornography. (I understand that there is a pornographic video which advertises itself as "Do Ask, Do Tell" and this should not be confused with my material at all.)

36)   But even if they were able to provide service for my site, I have to admit a bit of discomfort with using them. Neither of these companies have the reputation of, say, Visa or Mastercard. I do not know their privacy and security policies. (For example, will my users start receiving junk e-mail from hard-core pornography sites if they sign up for these services?) And I certainly do not feel confident that they will be a safe firewall between me and a federal prison sentence.

37)   The actual commercial volume on my site is too small at this time to make acceptance of credit cards economically sensible. A friend of mine who set up credit card charge ability on his Web site found that the minimum a bank or credit card verification company charges is $50 a month plus transaction fees. If I passed charges like these on to my users, it would kill access to my site, since most users only access my materials for brief periods for social or political research and would find the costs prohibitive. And I cannot afford to take on these charges myself. I do not yet make a profit from the site, although I hope to some day after retirement with enough effort. I am afraid that with the requirements of the Act, I will be forced to either further self-censor or shut the site down completely.

38)   I believe that the High Productivity Production site, along with other small sites containing political speech, is very important. With desktop publishing and the World Wide Web, a single person such as myself can compete with well-established and well-funded organizations and make an impact upon public debate of important and timely issues. My site is valuable because there is no outside supervision and I owe no loyalty to large organizations to support other groups' issues so they will support mine. In my case, there is no point in operating a site that does not have some moderately adult content that is conveniently accessed and searched by researchers.

I declare and affirm under penalty of perjury that the foregoing is true and correct.

Dated: _____   _____

JOHN WILLIAM BOUSHKA

(The physical format of this affidavit has been modified and shortened for book publication as reference material for the convenience of the reader.)

Appendix 2:

Outline for a Classroom Presentation of Fundamental Rights

CATEGORIES OF RIGHTS

- Original Rights
- Fundamental Rights
- Social Rights
- Family Rights
- Collective Rights
- Expressive Rights

ORIGINAL *RIGHT*

A right clearly spelled out in the Constitution of the United States or in any of the amendments.

EXAMPLES OF ORIGINAL RIGHTS

- Freedom of speech
- Freedom of religion
- Freedom of the press
- Don't have to quarter soldiers

- **Right to bear arms**
- **No unreasonable search and seizure**
- **No self-incrimination**
- **No double jeopardy**
- **Due process of law (procedural and substantive)**
- **Trial by jury (civil and criminal)**
- **No cruel or unusual punishment**
- ***Writ of habeas corpus***
- **No *ex post facto law***
- **No involuntary servitude**
- **Equal protection of the law**
- **Life, liberty, property**
- **When voting is set up by a state, no discrimination**

FUNDAMENTAL RIGHT

A right which may be original or may be established by long cultural or judicial tradition, as essential to life, liberty, property, or the pursuit of happiness. A fundamental right limits the power of the federal government and, according to the incorporation doctrine of the Fourteenth Amendment, the powers of individual states when a conflict exists with the purported right. Generally, a government must pass strict scrutiny to abridge a fundamental right, and this notion is called "substantive due process."

EXAMPLES OF FUNDAMENTAL RIGHTS

- **Right of privacy (or the "right to be left alone")**
- **To become a parent and have a family**
- **To vote (?)**
- **Freedom of speech**
- **Freedom of religion**
- **Freedom of the press**

- Don't have to quarter soldiers
- Right to bear arms
- No unreasonable search and seizure
- No self-incrimination
- No double jeopardy
- Due process of law (procedural or substantive)
- Trial by jury (civil and criminal)
- No cruel or unusual punishment
- *Writ of habeas corpus*
- No *ex post facto law*
- No involuntary servitude
- Equal protection of the law
- Life, liberty, property
- Right of publicity and "freedom" from libel (as a "property right")
- When voting is set up by a state, no discrimination

SOCIAL RIGHT

A purported right that requires that a government set up the facility to exercise the right, usually with public or tax expenditures, sometimes with intentional sacrifices by others.

Examples:

- Public education
- Universal health care (Europe, Canada)
- Eldercare
- Subsidies for parents or families (Europe)
- Voting (!)

Some writers call these "affirmative rights"

COLLECTIVE RIGHT

A right that applies more to people acting together in a group than to individuals acting on their own.

The main example is the right to bear arms.

Other examples: Freedom of assembly, petition, even freedom of the press

EXPRESSIVE RIGHT

The right to promote oneself; the right to publish.

The main example is individualized free speech, the right to become a town crier or mount a soap box and draw attention to oneself.

But property rights are, in general, expressive rights.

Another important example is the purported right to choose a consenting adult as an intimate partner or "significant other." The Supreme Court, in *Bowers v. Hardwick* (1986), turned down the idea that all private sexuality constituted a fundamental right.

PROBLEMS WITH SOME FUNDAMENTAL RIGHTS

• Balance with general public welfare or safety
• Balance with social justice or fairness

PROBLEMS WITH SOME EXPRESSIVE RIGHTS

• They are particularly "human"
• Some people don't "pay their dues" (don't have responsibility for others besides themselves)
(draft, national service, forced volunteerism)

• Dependable social institutions (the nuclear family) are challenged
• Underlying social conflict over the universal importance of having and raising children as a motivator.

TURF!!

Creativity ——————————————————→
←——————————————————Professionalism

Self-Promotion ————————————————→
←—————— Family ————————————————→
←——————————————Serving needs of others

[1] George Soros, *The Crisis of Global Capitalism: Open Society Endangered* (New York, Public Affairs, 1998).

[2] *Do Ask, Do Tell* and *Our Fundamental Rights*. For hardcopy orders, visit http://www.hppub.com/obtain.thm. (or amazon.com, bn.com, or for DADT iuniverse.com). My own original proposal for a constitutional amendment appears at http://www.hppub.com/rights.htm and my original argument for this proposal, dating back to the August 1996 Quill (published by Gays and Lesbians for Individual Liberty) appears at http://www.hppub.com/glil3.htm. That essay was the very first essay of mine to be posted on the World Wide Web, then on home.aol.com in 1996, as this was one of AOL's first formats for personal publisher.

[3] David Boaz, *Libertarianism, A Primer* and *The Libertarian Reader* (New York, The Free Press, 1997).

[4] Bill Boushka, *Do Ask, Do Tell*, Chapter 3, Section 04.

[5] These terms, **affirmative rights, social rights** and **entitlements** are all loaded words that have been used in various ways. Harold Spaeth and Edward Conrad Smith, in the Harper College Outline <u>The Constitution of the United States</u> (1991) provide a slightly different flavor to these terms. An "affirmative right" is supposed to be a right to have something from the government (or a right "received from government"). By comparison, most "constitutional rights are negative in that they protect persons from government action." (P. 47.) An example would be Medicare benefits. Generally, Spaeth uses the term "affirmative right" to be synonymous with entitlement, with a few additional cases, such as a constitutional right for an indigent person to be represented by counsel. Generally, the constitutional constraint upon entitlements is that they may not be implemented in a discriminatory manner by either the federal or by state or local governments (the states being constrained by the 14th Amendment). Even the right to vote is not "technically" a constitutional right in Spaeth's view; it is granted and controlled by states—an observation which may well prove relevant in the Bush appeal to the Supreme Court of the actions

by the Florida Supreme Court in November 2000. I think that a good word for a right granted by government through legislation would be simply **legislated right**, or even"**statutory right**. (And **original right** could be used in place of affirmative right; also the term **preordained** right has been used and, after all, the Declaration of Independence had used the term **inalienable** right.) In Chapter 4 of DADT I coined the term **substantive right** as a synonym for a fundamental right particularly when largely established through statute.

I think that you still can talk about free speech and self-defense as "affirmative rights" in that they are rights to "do something," although these are supposed to come from the Bill of Rights and not from government (and this gets sticky with the gun control issue). When I used the term, I felt that we needed a word that differentiates between liberty interests directly implied by the federal Bill of Rights and those liberty interests subsequently incorporated to the states by the 14th Amendment. The accepted term for the right to "do something" without interference from government seems, however, to be fundamental right, as the Supreme Court used the term in *Bowers v. Hardwick* (1986).

Spaeth is pointing out a very important notion. Certain capabilities and protections that we usually take for granted as rights really do have to be established by legislation, often at the state and local level. The right of a child to an education is established when a county sets up public schools and levies school taxes. Police protection is thought of as a right but technically is not and this observation is often used to emphasize the original (affirmative) right of an individual to defend himself, his family and property by bearing arms. Even freedom from de facto segregation is not itself a constitutional right, although courts (guided by the 14th Amendment) may generally prevent state and local governments from adopting legislation that actually causes *de facto* segregation.

Spaeth's comments explain the wording of constitutional amendments related to suffrage (15th for race and previous servitude, 19th for gender, 24th for not paying or inability to pay poll tax and 26th for age [if over 18]). These amendments provide that an already existing right to vote may not be infringed upon but the original right must be legislated by the state in which the individual resides (and in practice always is). Of course, this kind of reasoning has its own Catch-22. In the *Bush v. Gore* 2000 election before the Supreme Court, the issue of recounting after the date established in state law for a presidential election was held to violate the 14th Amendment equal protection clause, both in terms of changing a deadline after the fact but particularly in terms of differing subjective manual voting methods within a state. The local discretion in vote counting and recounting had not in and of itself been considered violate equal protection in the past.

Maybe a better example of a truly legislated right (or even a social right) is the right to organize (form labor unions) in the workplace, which must be established by federal and state laws (and may be limited by state and federal laws in some cases). This legislated right incorporates the right of labor to **collective bargaining**. However, some of these rights (like collective bargaining) are well established in human rights tradition, as declared in the 1948 Universal Declaration of Human Rights. On the other hand, collective bargaining, in particular, may be offset by state right-to- work laws.

Another example is a public education; the right to it must be established by the state or local legislation and government (and there could be state constitutions that guarantee this, but the federal Constitution does not; it would hold that equal protection may not be violated in providing it). One wonders if *Bush v. Gore* will some day cause uneven funding of public education (by local property taxes) to be seen as violating equal protection (this has been argued in the context of some state constitutions) as had once segregation. Far-fetched but not impossible.

Even marriage (outside of common-law marriage) could be looked upon as a legislated right (a relevant point to the same-sex marriage debate and the 1996 Defense of Marriage Act).

A welfare "safety net" has come to be regarded as a social right, especially by members of the Left who see poorer individuals as powerless against established interests that exploit them. Tom Palmer of the Cato Institute points out, in the context of opportunity costs, that welfare and public medical programs have pretty much eroded the "mutual aid" societies (like the Eastern Star and the Masons) that used to provide medical care and social services on a low-cost voluntary basis. Publicly funded health care replaced voluntary aid societies in Britain early in the 20th Century when the medical community say the government as a vehicle for establishing a cartel. A resurrection of "mutual aid" societies could help alleviate the eldercare crisis, and ironically this is now being tried in China!

Palmer also points out that individual rights imply obligations: individuality implies a personal space that may not be intruded upon without consent and that the obtaining of consent (in conjunction with "responsibility") is itself an expressive and life-enriching activity. Even some original rights (as used above) imply obligations. For example, the right to a jury trial (6th and 7th Amendments) implies an **obligation** for other citizens to serve on juries (although jury duty could be made voluntary).

It is well to reiterate the fundamental debate over the Bill of Rights in the late 18th Century. If you limited the powers of the federal government to a specified list, why did you need a "bill of rights" if you ran the risk of implying that unspecified rights were not protected. That's why we have a Ninth Amendment (expanding upon unenumerated rights) and Tenth Amendment (limiting unenumerated powers). After the Civil War, former Confederacy President Jefferson Davis was eventually released from prison at Fort Monroe when the government was afraid to test his contention, that states had a right to secede inasmuch as the Constitution does not give Congress or the Executive an enumerated power to stop them, in the Supreme Court—after all that carnage.

[6] Amitai Etzioni, *The Limits of Privacy* (New York: Basic Books, 1999).

[7] *Harvard Law Review,* Dec. 15, 1890, Vol. 4 No. 5.
http://www.lawrence.edu/fac/boardmaw/Privacy_brand_warr2.html

[8] See note 5, where the development of the concept of "social rights" is welded to Spaeth's notion of "affirmative rights."

[9] David Kluge, A People's Guide to the United States Constitution (Citadel, 1994), pp. 150-155, including Justice David Souter's remarks.
Also, John R. Vile, "Constitutional Amending Process," from *The Oxford Companion to the Supreme Court,* edited by Kermit Hall (Oxford University Press, 1992), pp. 179-181. Vile has written several books on this topic, as are visible on Amazon.com. Vile, in *Contemporary Questions Surrounding the Constitutional Amending Process* (London: Praeger, 1993) summarizes another work, *We the People: Foundations,* by Bruce Ackerman, in which a third "Article V" style method is proposed: a president in his second term submits and amendment to Congress, which may by a 2/3 majority in each house send the amendment to popular vote in two successive presidential elections where 3/5 majorities would be required. Ackerman wants to formally expand

the Bill of Rights by such a process, probably to include some "social rights" as included among "inalienable rights," or "fundamental rights."

10 See note 6

11 One could also decompose the constitutional amending process can be functionally decomposed into four distinct threads: (1) Congress proposes an amendment by a 2/3 majority; 3/4 of the states ratify by simple majority votes in their state legislatures. This is the method most often used. (2) Congress proposes an amendment by a 2/3 majority; then 3/4 of the states ratify by state constitutional conventions. This method was used to pass the prohibition amendment. (3) An amendment is proposed by a state-mandated constitutional convention and ratified by 3/4 of the legislatures of the several states. This method was used for to establish Constitution itself as a successor to the Articles of Confederation, and generates talk of "runaway conventions." (4) An amendment is proposed by a federal constitutional convention and ratified by 3/4 of the states through state constitutional conventions. This method still has never been used.

12 Morton Kaplan, "Tribe and Scalia on the Constitution, A Third View," *The World and I*, April 1999, pp 311-331. Kaplan provides a lot of discussion on the flag burning amendment and abortion issues. The *Oxford Companion to the Supreme Court* provides discussions of interpretivism and non-interpretivism (Gary L. McDowell), textualism and constitutional interpretation (Philip Bobbit) and judicial activism (McDowell).

13 AOL used to run an Academic Assistance Center. It discussed "the formal and informal ways to amend the Constitution.
Another source here is Eugene W. Hickock, Jr. (editor) *The Bill of Rights: Original Meaning and Current Understanding* (University of Virginia, 1991), particularly the essays by Charles Cooper and Edward Ehler, "Original Intnet and the Ninth Amendment." Ehler interrupts an otherwise fine conservative essay with the astonishing statement, "Homosexuality, no less than slavery, is incompatible with the principles of republicanism" when discussing *Bowers v. Hardwick* and the right to privacy. Many of the founding fathers (even including James Madison at first) resisted the idea of a Bill of Rights on the theory that its existence would imply that non-enumerated

rights remain removable at the mercy of federal government. Jacob G. Hornbergerm in "Do Rights Come from the Constitution," *Minnesota Libertarian*, July 1999, p. 11, presents the notion of the Bill of Rights as really a "Bill of Prohibitions" upon the federal and state governments. Mr. Hornberger is president of the Future of Freedom foundation.

[14] As of 2002, the possibility remains that the Supreme Court may revisit sodomy laws with respect to the Texas statute.

[15] *Do Ask Do Tell*, Chapter 3, Section 05.

[16] Dirk Selland, "Will Maryland Enter the Twenty-First Century in the Right Direction by Rescinding its Ancient Sodomy Statutes," *Tulane University Law Review*, p. 688.

[17] In April 25, 1999 Pastor Paul Graetz at All God's Children Metropolitan Community Church in Minneapolis commented, "Not everyone has the same opportunity for equality." Some libertarians maintain that federal income taxes are unconstitutional despite the 16th Amendment (see Irwin Schiff's The Federal Mafia, Freedom Press, 1994). Along the lines of social rights discussed above, there was in 1999 a proposed Constitutional amendment asserting the right to health care. "All citizens of the United States shall have equal access to basic and essential care." This would have the effect, at the constitutional level rather than the statutory level, of requiring the forced redistribution of wealth. Of course, an individually competitive society can run up against a stone wall for affording health care for older citizens who, left to their own devices or even their own families, present greater health insurance risks and anti-selection. In a similar spirit, President Clinton once proposed making parents a "protected class," which, as a matter of law, would make non-parents effectively second class citizens.

[18] James Q. Wilson and Leon Klass debate, "To Clone or Not to Clone," *The American Enterprise*, March/April 1999, p. 67.

19 Scott Kiloby, "Boy Scouts, You Can't Sleep in my Tent" at http://www.queer-soup.com; Gays and Lesbians for Individual Liberty, amicus brief before the Supreme Court in James Dale v. Boy Scouts of America; Richard Sincere, "Pro-Gary Ruling in New Jersey Hurts Gay Rights," *Wall Street Journal*, Aug. 11, 1999, p. A18, also various writings by Paul Varnell and Bruce Bawer.

20 Orlando Patterson. "The Liberal Millennium: What Liberalism Still Needs to Learn about Freedom." *The New Republic*, Nov. 8, 1999, p. 54. See also Patterson's *Freedom: Freedom in the Making of Western Culture* (New York: Basic Books, 1991).

21 Alex Alexiev, "The End of an Alliance: It's time to tell the House of Saud goodbye," *National Review*, Oct. 28, 2002, p. 38.

22 Tamim Ansary, "An Afghan-American speaks: You can't bomb us back into the Stone Age. We're already there. But you can start a new world war, and that's exactly what Osama bin Laden wants." http://www.salon.com/news/feature/2001/09/14/afghanistan/

23 Eyad Sarraj, "Why We Blow Ourselves Up: A Palestinian doctor explains why so many of his people want to be martyrs," *Time*, April 5, 2002, p. 39.

24 I brought this point up at panel discussion at a screening of *Peace of Mind* at a Jewish Community Center and was met with an ambivalent response as to the historical role of property rights in the region.

25 The correct Arabic term for militant political expansion for religious purposes is supposed to be "kazra," not "jihad." The Koran is probably even more open to interpretation than the Bible, because Arabic lacks specificity in terms of time relationships, state of being and possession when compared to modern languages.

26 Rose Wilder Lane. *Islam and the Discovery of Freedom*, introduction and commentary by Imad-ad-Dean Ahmad, Ph. D., Amana, Minaret of Freedom Institute, 1997. Also see http://www.minaret.org and http://www.amermuslim.org.

27 See Koran 5:33, 8:37, 9:73, 17:16, 47:4.
These verses are cited by the Jewish Task Force and are widely circulated on the Internet.

28 Yahiya, Emerick, *The Complete Idiot's Guide to Understanding Islam*, Alpha Press, 2002.

29 For example, George Gilder, *Men and Marriage* (New Orleans: Pelican, 1986).

30 Jonathan Rauch, "The Mullahs and the Postmodernists," *The Atlantic Monthly*, Jan. 2002, p. 21.

31 Alexander Stille, "Virgins or Raisins: Scholars dare to re-interpret the Qur'an," The New York Times, March 20, 2002, discusses the anger that intellectual and historical investigations of the source and authenticity of the Koran as scripture (as interpreted by some Muslims) can bring. Salman Rushdie, recall, lived under threat of assassination for his book *Satanic Verses*.

32 David Brooks, "Among the Bourgeoisophobes: Why the Europeans and Arabs, each in their own way, hate America and Israel", *The Weekly Standard*, April 15, 2002, p. 20.

33 Dinesh D'Souza, "Osama's Brain: Meet Sayyid Qutb, intellectual father of the anti-Western jihad." *The Weekly Standard*, April 29, 2002, p. 16. See also note 27. See also his new book *What's So Great About America*, Regnery, 2002.

34 All of these quotes in "New York September Eleven TwoThousandOne" published by the Robin Hood Relief Fund.

35 Noam Chomksy, *9/11*, Seven Stories Press (Canada), 2001.

36 Dr. Bruce G. Blair, "What If the Terrorists Go Nuclear," Center For Defense Information, Terrorism Project, Oct. 1, 2001. http://www.cdi.org/terrorism/nuclear.cfm

37 James Rosen, "Loose nukes in Russia create a new urgency: Anti-U.S. groups may have dangerously easy access to nuclear materials," Minneapolis *Star Tribune*, July 8, 2002. Rosen also reports the 1996 claim by Gen Alexander Lebed (formerly a security advisor to Boris Yeltsin) about the 84 missing suitcase nukes, but also reports that today both Russian and U.S. officials now deny this claim. An up-to-date objective documentary of the security controls on Russian nuclear, biological and chemical weapons and on unaccounted-for losses seems to be in order. Frontline would be a good start, but this seems to call for a feature-length film.

38 David Westphal, "Dirty bombs: The New Nuclear Threat," Minneapolis *Star Tribune*, July 7, 2002. This article warns of the possibility that terrorists could build a crude nuclear bomb and investigates dirty bombs in a sidebar, "Dirty Bombs are potent psychological weapon," on p. A13. Even a very small dirty device like a truck bomb with a small amount of cesium or cobalt (possibly stolen from medical supplies or wastes) could present enormous problems in assessing downstream health and cancer risks and whether the public could live with a slight or moderate increase in cancer deaths. The seven nations with nuclear weapons are the U.S., Russia, Great Britain, France, Israel, China, India, and Pakistan. There is controversy over whether Pakistan has actually deployed any small nukes. Iran, Iraq, North Korea, and Libya are all known to be attempting or to have attempted to acquire nuclear weapons. Another important issue in this issue of the *Star Tribune* is "Iraq likely to use taboo weapons: Iraqi leader has little to lose if U.S. invades to remove him" by John Hendren of the *Los Angeles Times*.

39 Michael A. Levi and Henrcy C. Kelly, "Weapons of Mass Disruption: Radiological terror weapons could blow radioactive dust through cities, causing panic, boosting cancer rates and forcing costly cleanups," *Scientific American*, Nov. 2002, p. 76.
Steven Johnson, "Stopping Loose Nukes: How an atomic wall sill save America's cities," *Wired*, Nov. 2002m p. 162,

40 But Peter Richmond, in "How to Build a Suitcase Nuke: It's quite simple, really. And more than one expert believes Al Qaeda has done it," in *Gentleman's Quarterly*, Feb. 2002, presents a sobering dissent to any such

reassuring complacency. This magazine announces now on its cover "Buy this magazine or the terrorists have won." Richmond takes up the question as to whether "they" would "use it" if they have it, and it is important to note that Al Qaeda and similar groups usually do not make demands with their attacks. President George W. Bush alluded to the blackmail possibility in his "State of the Union" address on January 28, 2002. It should be remembered that Gore Vidal had warned the public about terrorism in the August 2002 *Vanity Fair*, in expressing dissatisfaction over the investigation of Timothy McVeght (#1).

41 Massimo Calabresi, and Romesh Ratnesar, "Can We Stop the Next Attack," *Time*, March 11, 2002.

42 Philip Shenon, "Qaeda Leader Said to Report A-Bomb Plans," *The New York Times*, April 23, 2002, p. 9. This logline is misleading; a dirty bomb is not an atomic bomb.
Ben Brandt, "Weapons of Mass Destruction: Not a Doomsday Review," *The American Experience Quarterly*, Fall 2002.

43 John B. Roberts (II), "The Nuclear Bomb Squad: Could they halt an attack in time?" *Reader's Digest*, May 2002, p. 74. See also earlier *Reader's Digest* pieces: Susan Freinkel, "The Unthinkable: The most worrisome threats on the home front—and what you can do," Feb. 2002, p. 61, and Alexis Jetter, "What If…an outbreak of smallpox threatens to spiral out of control? Can we contain it?" p. 67

44 Thomas Gale Moore [of Hoover Institute] "How to Reduce Terrorism: Bring American Troops Home," San Jose Mercury News, June 11, 2002. At one point Moore writes: "According to a Zogby International Poll released on April 11, a majority of people in the five Arab countries and three non-Arab Muslim states view our freedom and our democracy with favor. But overwhelmingly, they disapprove of our policies toward Arab nations and the Palestinians. Kuwait, for example, which we rescued from Iraq, liked our freedom and democracy by 58 percent to 39 percent, but only 6 percent viewed our policies favorably and a huge 88 percent disapproved of our policies in the Middle East. Other Muslim countries had almost identical views. And this poll was taken before Israel sent its military into the West Bank!" Indeed, a

few people consider this essay of mine to be promotion of conservative propaganda so I will certainly state and respect opposing views. Are the attacks, as
Chomsky hints, somehow our desserts for past imperialism or foreign political opportunism? (Is that propaganda?) Again, there is this question about
peaceful coexistence of authoritarianism with freedom and whether the radical militant faction of the Muslim world can maintain its separate planet.

[45] President George W. Bush, State of the Union Address, January 28, 2002.

[46] Mark Miller and Daniel Klaidman, "Hunt for the Anthrax Killer," *Newsweek*,
Aug. 12, 2002 reports the searches by the FBI against a scientist as a person
of interest, near Fort Dietrich at Frederick, Md. It seems as thought the government has invited enormous media coverage on the basis of provocative circumstantial evidence (and there are cries to remember the mistakes in 1996
with Olympic Park when the FBI misidentified someone back in 1996 in
connection with an incident at the Atlanta Olympics). The government even
seized a hard drive in that person's apartment with an unpublished novel
about bioterrorism. It is not supposed to create legal risk to write anything
until the writing is "published" or intentionally shown to someone else. How
will publishers feel about terrorist-associated materials after a seizure like this?
(The Patriot Act would not have made it illegal for an employee to publish a
novel unless classified material were disclosed, although that's also a gray
area.) It is possible that a foreign terrorist could manipulate circumstantial
evidence to frame an ordinary American citizen.

[47] David Tell. "Remember Anthrax? The FBI seems to have no idea who sent it,
but won't let go of it's ;lone American' theory." *The Weekly Standard*, April 29,
2002, p. 22.

[48] *Time*, May 21, 2002. http://www.time.com/time/covers/1101020603/
story.html This letter would be in the public domain. The simple text is at
http://hppub.com/hpdadt/rowley.htm

[49] Michael Isikoff and Daniel Klaidman, "The Hijackers We Let Escape,"
Newsweek, June 3, 2002. Jonathan Alter has an article in the same issue about
the level of information that should be circulated in public (ranging from the
"terrorism for dummies" sites to legitimate self-protection information).

Again, the government's warning levels (Red, Orange, Yellow, Blue, Green) from high to low—they don't follow the spectrum—correspond roughly to the DEFCON alerts.

50 Electronic Frontier Foundation. http://www.eff.org/Privacy/Surveillance/ Terrorism_militias/20011031_eff_usa_patriot_analysis.html

51 Matthew Rothschild, "The New McCarthyism," *The Progressive*, Jan., 2002, p. 18.

52 *Ibid.*

53 Jim McTague, "Wanted: Wyatt Earps," *Barron's*, March 4, 2002.

54 Paul Wallich, "Who's Who: Can Digital Technology Prevent Identity Theft," *Scientific American*, July 2002, p. 19.

55 Adam Liptak, Neil A. Lewis, and Benjamin Weiser, "After Sept. 11, a Legal Battle on the Limits of Civil Liberty," *The New York Times*, Aug. 4, 2002.

56 Walt Brasch, "The Patriot Act and Free Speech: The Fiction Behind National Security" (white paper). http://www.counterpunch.org/braschfree speech.html

57 Holly Dolezalek and Dennis Muller, "Data Security Auditors, St. Paul Company focuses on Data Security," *Twin Cities Computer User*, July 2, 2002, p. 10.

58 Barton Gellman, "Cyber-Attacks by Al Qaeda Feared: Terrorists on Threshold of Using Internet as Tool of Bloodshed, Experts Say," *The Washington Post*, June 27, 2002.

59 The original article on this subject by Charles Moskos was :Now Do You Believe We Need a Draft" on November 2001 in the *Washington Monthly* (also the November 4, 2001 *Washington Post*). The counterpoint with Lawrence Korb appeared in the December 2001 *American Enterprise*, and "Reviving the Citizen Soldier" appeared in *The Public Interest*, Spring 2002.

[60] Charles Krauthammer, *Newsweek*, Oct. 2001, and many columns at http://www.washingtonpost.com/wp-dyn/opinion/columns/krauthammer-charles/ Kruathammer warned about the likelihood that the U.S. would be in a war with Iraq by the end of 2002.

[61] Frank Davies, "Doomsday threat grips Congress: How would it function in face of catastrophe?" *St. Paul Pioneer Press*, April 8, 2002. This article discusses some proposed constitutional amendments for succession, such as allowing governors to appoint interim members of the House of Representatives after a major catastrophe that caused casualties in the House.

[62] Michael Scott Doran, "Long War in the Making: Somebody Else's Civil War," *Foreign Affairs*, Jan/Feb 2002.

[63] Rand Corporation (National Defense Research Institute). *Sexual Orientation and U.S. Military Personnel Policy: Options and Assessment*. (Los Angeles: Rand, 1993).

[64] Sebastian Junger, *Fire*, (New York: W. W. Norton, 2001).

[65] Marc Wolf, "Another American: Asking and Telling," *Political Stages: Plays that Shaped a Century* (edited by Emily Mann and David Roessel, Applause Books, 2002).

[66] Dixon Osburn and others, *Conduct Unbecoming: Eight Annual Report on Don't Ask, Don't Tell*, Servicemembers' Legal Defense Network, Washington, D.C., March 2002.

[67] *Smallville* (2001), series on Warner Brothers cable and available on Video and DVD from Warner Brothers.

[68] Tom Shanker, "Who Will Fight This War?" *The New York Times*, Sept. 30, 2001.

[69] Tim Cavanaugh, "Service Economy: First-draft Suggestions for a Real Draft Proposal," *Reason*, Feb. 2001, p. 21.

70 Jim Thompson and Mike Woodward, "Hot Carrers in a Cool Market: Ask Not What Business Can Do for You but What You Can Do for Business," *Computer User*, Jan. 2002, p. 13.

71 The TSA has, as of summer 2002, started hiring screeners with a great sense of urgency, presumably to comply with new federal laws. So now Moskos could be right; it could be very difficult to staff the available screening and supervisory positions with properly experienced individuals.

72 Vist http://www.airsafe.com/issues/security/screener.htm
"Requirements for Airport Security Screeners"
home page http://www.airsafe.com
Here is the Transportation Security Administration's web reference on job qualifications (as of August 2002):
http://www.tsa.gov/employment_opps/tss.shtm
The Transportation Security Administration is part of the Department of Transportation.

73 There have been some controversies about pat-down searches, but the DOT/TSA (Transportation Security Administration) does **not** have a "don't ask don't tell" policy or ban on gays for security screening jobs on the theory that passengers would object or perceive an invasion of privacy. I have attended one of the assessments, found the procedure to be moderately regimented, with applicants not allowed to leave the center while being tested. Presently, the TSA expects applicants to interpret the personnel policies stated on its web site literally without exception, somewhat in a military-like manner. Applicants who would be uncomfortable with the possibility of having to perform pat-downs should not apply, although they are not specifically asked about this.

74 Richard Goldstein, "Attack of the Gaycons: Fighting the Gay Right," *The Nation*, July 1, 2002.

75 Chris Bull, "The New Face of Gay Conservatives," *The Advocate*, Apr. 16, 2002, p. 43. This story focused upon Mass, lieutenant governor candidate Patrick Guerriero.

76 Dinesh D'Souza, *What's So Great About America* (Washington: Regenery, 2002), especially Chapter 5, "When Virtue Loses All Her Loveliness: Freedom and Its Abuses."

77 Paul Rosenfels. *Homosexuality: The Psychology of the Creative Process* with Introduction by Dean Hannotte. New York: Ninth Street Center, 1972/1986.

78 Joe Babcock. *The Tragedy of Miss Geneva Flowers*. Minneapolis: Closet Case Books, 2002.

79 Bob Weinstein, "Mainframes are still around, and so is the demand for programmers," Tech Watch, King Features Syndicate, *Minneapolis Star Tribune*, April 28, 2002, page J1.

80 Julia King, "Mainframe skills, pay at a premium," *Computerworld*, March 4, 2002.

81 Here is the URL for it: http://www.hipaaplus.com/abouthippa.htm

82 Barbara Ehrenreich, *Nickel and Dimed: On (Not) Getting By in America* (New York: Henry Holt, 2001), provides a chilling look at minimum wage work in "real jobs," manual labor that the rest of us depend up shamelessly.

83 Jim Thompson, "Hot Careers in a Cool Market," *Computer User*, January 2002.

84 Robert McGarvey, "On Site from Afar: Distance Training Is Changing the Way IT Managers Keep Employee Skills Fresh," *Computer User*, July 2002.

85 Bob Weinstein, Tech Watch, "Enlist in Web firm AIT's boot camp and be all that you can be," *Star Tribune*, Aug. 4, 2002.

86 *Miller v. California* (1973) sets forth a similar three-prong test for obscenity and relies upon community standards. "There is no constitutional barrier under *Miller* to prohibiting communications that are obscene in some communities under local standards even though they are not obscene in others."

[87] *Hamling v. United States* (1974). "This Court, however, rejected Justice Brennans argument that the federal mail statute unconstitutionally compelled speakers choosing to distribute materials on a national basis to tailor their messages to the least tolerant community: The fact that distributors of allegedly obscene materials may be subjected to varying community standards in the various federal judicial districts into which they transmit the materials does not render a federal statute unconstitutional."

[88] *Sable Communications of California v. FCC* (1989). *Sable* addressed the constitutionality of 47 U.S.C. 223(b) (1982 ed., Supp. V), a statutory provision prohibiting the use of telephones to make obscene or indecent communications for commercial purposes. The petitioner in that case, a dial-a-porn operator, challenged, in part, that portion of the statute banning obscene phone messages. Like respondents here, the dial-a-porn operator argued that reliance on community standards to identify obscene material impermissibly compelled message senders to tailor all their messages to the least tolerant community. *492 U.S., at 124.* Relying on *Hamling*, however, this Court once again rebuffed this attack on the use of community standards in a federal statute of national scope: There is no constitutional barrier under *Miller* to prohibiting communications that are obscene in some communities under local standards even though they are not obscene in others. *If Sables audience is comprised of different communities with different local standards, Sable ultimately bears the burden of complying with the prohibition on obscene messages. 492 U.S., at 125126*

[89] Tracey Baker, "The Dark Side of the 'Net," *Smart Computing*, August 2002, p. 40. Baker mentions at one site, http://www.quova.com, is already offering software to determine the location of a client computer viewing a site. It is not yet clear how affordable or practical this is for a small business.

[90] There are many sources of this text, such as http://www.aclj.org/ussc/cppa/index.asp

91 Steve Silberman, "The United States of America v. Adam Vaughn," *Wired*, October 2002, p. 126.

92 The Libertarian Party of Minnesota publishes this periodical; visit www.lpmn.org.

0-595-26059-4

www.ingramcontent.com/pod-product-compliance
Lightning Source LLC
Chambersburg PA
CBHW061400280526
45784CB00001B/317